WHAT OTHERS ARE SAYING

"Personal Branding and Marketing Yourself is a must-read! The definition of the JOB is changing as we shift from career employment to career employability. It is no longer just what you know, but how best to tell the world what it is you know. Allen's book will take professionals in all stages of their careers through a discovery process on how best to capture and promote what is unique about oneself – keys to maximizing one's potential."

> — Bob Kelleher, Bestselling Author,
> Louder Than Words, 10 Practical Employee Engagement Steps That Drive Results and Chief Engagement Officer and Founder, The Employee Engagement Group

"Rita has encapsulated her personal branding philosophy and many years of coaching experience into a practical hands-on framework that will help you focus on the most important elements of building your personal brand."

> — V. Murray, HR Executive
> Financial Services

"This book provides insightful personal experiences, stories and guidelines to help prepare a person at any age and profession in digging deep to align your values to your career, how to market yourself as well as developing confidence by truly knowing your strengths. Utilize this book during and throughout your career, even when you are not looking for a job… It provides the 'how to' and is a must-read for all of us!"

> — Debbie Balaguer
> Regional Vice President of Sales
> STAT!Ref

"While I had been wary of applying the concept of 'branding' to my own professional life, I found Rita's approach convincing, refreshing, and applicable. Rita's '3P' process actively guides you in recognizing, defining, and articulating your authentic self. Rita's inclusion of clients' perspectives and experiences helps you see how different individuals have defined and celebrated their own personal brands."

— Kathleen Cronin, Former Vice President of Human Resources at a Boston area university

"As a GenXer rising up in my career, I found Balian Allen's book to be an incredibly useful tool with practical advice on using the Three Ps Technique as a roadmap to building one's personal brand as a successful career management strategy. Personal Branding and Marketing Yourself is engaging, empowering and a terrific read for anyone looking to build their brand at any career level."

— Ellen Keiley, President, National Assoc. of Women MBAs (Boston); Director of Business Development, Sherin and Lodgen LLP

"Having known Rita for several years, I've seen her as a dedicated practitioner, colleague, consultant and friend. She has applied her years of talent management experience, knowledge and research to writing this book as an effective guide to taking charge of your career for any and all professionals. Her book captures her ability to attract the attention of sizable audiences on a variety of related topics as well as conducting one-on-one exercises with a client reflecting how desirable her expertise is regarded."

— Bob Gatti, President, Gatti & Associates

Personal Branding
AND
Marketing Yourself

Personal Branding
AND
Marketing Yourself

THE "THREE Ps" MARKETING TECHNIQUE
AS A GUIDE TO CAREER EMPOWERMENT

RITA BALIAN ALLEN

BALIAN PUBLISHING CO.

Dedicated to
Jason and Jillian
for your love, inspiration and support,
allowing me to follow my passion
and be the best I can be.

PERSONAL BRANDING AND MARKETING YOURSELF
by Rita Balian Allen

Balian Publishing Co.
460 Totten Pond Road, Suite 110
Waltham, MA 02451

Unattributed quotations are by Rita Balian Allen.

Contents

About the Author

Rita Balian Allen is the president of Rita B. Allen Associates, a provider of career management consulting and coaching services for individuals and organizations representing a variety of industries including high technology, biotechnology, financial services, professional services, medical devices/pharmaceuticals, higher education, healthcare, not-for-profit, and retail/consumer products. With over twenty-five years human resources experience, her specialty areas include a variety of talent management offerings including executive coaching, leadership development, management training and career development. Previously, she held roles as Vice President of Marketing and Search Services with Gatti & Associates, and human resources positions with C.R. Bard, Inc., BTU International and Unitrode Corporation.

Rita has a successful track record partnering with management to align Human Resources initiatives with business strategies. Throughout her career, she has developed strong competencies in organizational design and structuring, leadership/talent coaching and development, team building, change management, staffing/recruitment, employee relations and relationship building. As a search consultant, she worked closely with senior executives within a multitude of organizations to create and build effective Human Resources functions. She has advised, mentored, and coached executives, managers and employees throughout all phases of their careers and critical decision making processes.

Rita holds an MS in Leadership and a BS in Business Administration from Northeastern University. Rita currently serves as a member of the board of directors for More Than Words and is a former board member of The Boston Club and the Association of Career Professionals International – New England, where she served as President. She is also an active member of other professional associations, a frequent speaker at events, the author of several articles and a monthly column and blog, Rita's Career Corner, on the Global Business Hub section of Boston.com. Rita is an adjunct faculty member and Lecturer at Northeastern University and Bentley University. She was voted one of the top ten executive coaches by Women's Boston Business Journal, is certified in a variety of assessment tools and is fluent in Armenian.

Rita B. Allen Associates is located in Waltham, MA, 781-890-6803, www.ritaballenassociates.com.

Acknowledgements

There have been so many people who have inspired, guided, and supported me in this book writing endeavor. A deep note of gratitude, thankfulness and appreciation to the following individuals for sharing their personal stories and/or offering their advice, time, and help:

Charlie Anderson	Debra Kennedy
Debbie Balaguer	Dan Kraus
Carol Bergeron	Lynne Levesque
Mark Campbell	Patricia Manning
Lisa Clark	Susan Maupin
Cindy Connelly	Ed Melia
Patricia Cotter	Patricia Nardi
Kathe Cronin	Carol O'Donnell
Jodi Detjen	Anthony O'Reilly
Judy Dumont	Deborah Varao-Martin
Bob Gatti	V. Murray
Ken Hablow	Pete Vegeto
Ray Hilvert	Victoria Wang
Ellen Keiley	John Weaver
Bob Kelleher	

A special note of thanks to Liz Batchelder, my editor and graphic designer, for her help and guidance throughout the publishing process. In addition to her expertise, her energy, humor and enthusiasm made it fun. Not only have I gained an editor, but a colleague and friend!

A heartfelt thanks to my dear family and friends as well as the colleagues, both personal and professional, who encouraged me to write this book in addition to supporting me throughout my life and career. Your kind words have helped me more than you realize. Thank you to Tim for many years of partnership and help in many aspects of our lives. Last, but not least, I thank my incredible children, Jason and Jillian, for their ongoing, unconditional love, support, and faith in me, for humoring me when I have peppered them with quotes and "mom-isms" throughout their childhood and well into adulthood; for being my rocks and pushing me gently but strongly; and for always being there for me! You have made me so proud and filled with appreciation for being so lucky to be your mother! On a final note, I want to remember and honor my parents, who were my biggest fans and continue to inspire me. Although they are not here to enjoy this achievement with me, I know they are proud of me and that all of my life's good fortune is due to the strong foundation of faith, confidence, unconditional love and selfless generosity they bestowed upon me. I thank God for all of my blessings! Stay positive and be happy – words I have grown to live by!

Introduction

Regardless of age, regardless of position, regardless of the business we happen to be in, all of us need to understand the importance of branding. We are CEOs of our own companies: Me Inc. To be in business today, our most important job is to be head marketer for the brand called You.[1]

~ TOM PETERS
AUTHOR, SPEAKER, AND MANAGEMENT THOUGHT LEADER

Everyone has different points of their lifetime and career when a light bulb goes on and a revelation occurs that can be quite jolting. One of those jolts for me occurred in 1988 as I was transitioning from one job to another in the field of corporate human resources. As I was in the thick of this process, I realized that more often than not, we do not see ourselves as a "commodity" to be "marketed." We may know how to be very methodical, strategic and planful in our roles at work, but how about in managing our own careers?

I had graduated from business school with eight years of experience under my belt at that point, but I had not taken the time to do due diligence in relation to my own career planning. The success I had achieved up to that point was a product of timing and circumstances rather than deliberate planning and execution. Now that I had a strong foundation of experience and was in the process of a transition, the light bulb went on making it clear to me that it was time to take charge of my career rather than being a passenger along for the ride! For the next two decades, I not only empowered myself to take charge, I spent my career assisting other professionals to do the same.

When we hear the term marketing, we likely think of products, services and commodities. How about ourselves? Most people are not comfortable talking about themselves this way. Even more importantly, most people are not **prepared** to talk about themselves in this way – **packaging** their talents and accomplishments, showcasing them and **presenting** their value inside their organization as well as out in their profession, industry or community.

---

1 Peters, Tom (1197). "The Brand Called You." Online. Available HTTP: fastcompany.com/28905/brand-called-you. (Accessed January 27, 2014.)

Marketing ourselves is an essential ingredient to successfully manage our careers. It may sound too deliberate or disingenuous, but in reality, **marketing ourselves can be, and should be, our most natural and sincere skill**. All it really entails is having an authentic conversation that is subtle and organic in representing what we have to offer and what we hope to achieve.

How do we develop ease, confidence and comfort with a task that is considered so difficult by so many? First, we need to **shift our mindset** to one that does not view marketing ourselves as a task, but as a required competency for empowering ourselves to execute a successful career management strategy. Strong leadership begins and ends with inner strength, and leadership is no longer only found in the "C Suite." Today, employees throughout organizations can be viewed as leaders, and staff increasingly grow into new roles. Supporting staff in becoming their own advocates, with the goal of building sustainable careers, is a smart business strategy. The best way to attract and retain talent is to enable them

> We need to shift our mindset to one that does not view marketing ourselves as a task, but as a required competency for empowering ourselves to execute a successful career management strategy.

to reach their utmost potential and unleash the leadership capabilities that are valued throughout all levels of an organization today.

Marketing ourselves allows us to establish our niche, our differentiators, our value-add, and the worth that we have to offer. Defining and creating our *personal brand*, articulating it and then enhancing it is part of the marketing process. Marketing ourselves is a core competency that can become so effortless and second-nature that we do not even realize we are doing it.

Let's begin with a **vision exercise** to illustrate the importance of developing the core competency of marketing ourselves. Fast forward: it is **15 years into the future**. You have been invited to speak at an industry event because of your accomplishments and contributions throughout your career. What does that vision look like for you?

What do you want to be known for? Visualize what you want your "personal brand" to be in 15 years. Give this some thought and then answer the following questions:

- Was that difficult or easy?
- Do you know your worth?
- Can you define your personal brand?

- How easily can you articulate that brand?

- Do you actively work on enhancing your brand?

If you are like most people, you may have found this exercise a little daunting or overwhelming. Many people do not think that far in advance and try to deal with the current day, the here and now. However, the best way to equip ourselves for the career challenges we will inevitably face is to recognize our contributions and continuously work on enhancing and marketing our brand within our chosen fields. *We all need to have a mission for our career and specific goals we want to accomplish.* Without a plan, we do not have direction or any criteria for accountability. Creating this vision for ourselves is the beginning of creating a plan.

Now let's rewind back to the current day and take a moment to reflect on all of the demands that we face: demands that we have no control over such as the economy, competition, specialization vs. generalization, changing demographics, generational and cultural differences, leadership expectations and capabilities, as well as the globalization of our marketplace. Within the landscape of all these growing demands and challenges, have you positioned yourself for success? How ready are you to put your best foot forward if faced with a promotional opportunity, board consideration, networking event, professional association membership, project leadership, job interviews, and/or other growth potential?

Contrary to popular opinion, successful careers do not just happen. They take a lot of planning and due diligence. One of the key areas that I apply in my coaching model with clients is around goal setting – personally and professionally. In fact, a study on goal setting conducted by Gail Matthews, PhD, at Dominican University demonstrated that writing one's goals down enhances goal achievement. The study provides empirical evidence for the effectiveness of three coaching tools: accountability, commitment and writing down one's goals.[2]

In our global marketplace there is and always will be demand for accomplished, results-driven professionals with a proven track record who can add value. Only you can manage your career. Having a solid plan for yourself with specific goals and objectives is the best way to start the process, which involves defining, identifying, creating, building, articulating and enhancing your personal brand! Understanding the overlap of our personal brand and our company brand is also important to be able to recognize and distinguish the differences.

2　Matthews, Gail. "Goals Research Summary." Online. Available HTTP: dominican.edu/academics/ahss/undergraduate-programs-1/psych/faculty/fulltime/gailmatthews/researchsummary2.pdf. (Accessed January 27, 2014.)

THE "THREE Ps"
MARKETING TECHNIQUE

Preparation
DEFINE AND IDENTIFY BRAND

Packaging
CREATE AND BUILD BRAND

Presentation
ARTICULATE AND ENHANCE BRAND

Going hand in hand with the Three Ps, there are three practices shared by individuals who successfully carve out careers that are satisfying, rewarding and fulfilling. Think of people you know who have effectively created their brand and gone on to accomplish great things. We all know individuals like this with whom we've worked and/ or had the pleasure of being friends. There are a few good examples of these folks that we all know – Bill Gates, Sonia Sotomayor, Albert Einstein, Oprah Winfrey, Tom Brady, Vera Wang, Jack Welch, Tony Robbins, Barbara Corcoran, and Walt Disney to name a few. What do they all have in common? Three things: they know what they have to offer, they know what they want and they know how to ask for it!

THREE COMMONALITIES OF SUCCESSFUL PROFESSIONALS

1. Know what they have to offer (Their value-add)

2. Know what they want (Have specific goals)

3. Know how to ask for it (Advocate effectively)

Many individuals may excel at one or two of these areas, but you want to be able to comfortably achieve all three in order to empower yourself to take charge of your career. So, how do we develop the core competency of marketing ourselves with ease, comfort and confidence? How do we achieve these three commonalities – knowing our value, knowing what we want, and knowing how to ask for it?

Personal branding and marketing ourselves is an essential core competency than can actually become so effortless and second nature that we do not even realize we are doing so. It begins and ends with self-awareness and inner strength – it's about tapping into our utmost aspirations and potential. It is about empowering ourselves and being in the driver's seat rather than sitting in the back seat going along for the ride as an observer. It is a process that is ongoing and continuous throughout our careers – not something you do once and stop.

Many people feel overwhelmed by the activities and requirements of this process, or worse, end up avoiding it completely. It is challenging, but in the end, it truly is exhilarating! Once we achieve the discipline to create routines for ourselves, we will also establish ongoing behaviors that we are committed to maintaining, especially when we reap the rewards. It's also important to note that this process is not something to do without some formal or informal support and guidance from others.

Think about it: has anything that has yielded tremendous results ever been easy? I believe the answer is no. The most challenging experiences that are most memorable and satisfying are the ones that require us to stretch our thinking and tap into talents we might not have known we had. Managing our career is one of those experiences that is a journey with many peaks and valleys, and will require us to navigate crossroads, forks, dead ends, and new, exciting, untraveled roads. It requires us to stop along the way, reevaluate, take leaps of faith, and remind ourselves that the journey has no end. In order to know our personal brand and market ourselves, we need to walk through this process continuously and regularly.

Developing this core competency can be a rich and enlightening process. Because I know how difficult it can be, I set out to provide resources and support in this book: tips, tools, techniques and strategies for using my Three Ps Technique as a guide to career empowerment. I encourage you to use this book as a guide, manual, and workbook that you will review and revisit throughout your whole career. It is not a book that will be read from cover to cover in one sitting and then filed away. You will need time to think, reflect, and process in between sections. You will need time to complete activities, exercises and worksheets. I envision that you will end up with lots of notes, highlights, bookmarks, and Post-Its on these pages... and that you will keep it close by as a quick and handy reference. Remember, not only will you be asking yourself questions that force you to look deep within – you will also have to answer them. It may seem at times to be a trying journey, but it is also a fulfilling one that will leave you empowered to take charge of your career.

Enjoy the journey!

Preparation

Define & Identify Your Brand

Life begins at the end of your comfort zone.

~ NEALE DONALD WALSCH

AUTHOR AND INSPIRATIONAL THINKER

Preparation is the most difficult and critical part of the process – the foundation on which your further efforts are built. It is a cumulative process, so if you do not spend the appropriate amount of time and effort on this first step, your packaging and presentation will suffer. You will not be ready to package and present yourself until you have thoroughly reflected, challenged and pushed yourself in all the directions necessary to truly assess your value, needs and desires. I refer to this as conducting your due diligence in a deliberate, methodical and strategic manner, much as you would for any other business endeavor. First, we need to embrace the concept that we are the ones responsible for "owning our careers" and not putting them in someone else's hands to shape, mold or preserve. It requires us to be the lead person in navigating our path with the assistance, support and guidance of others. This requires us to know the talents we offer, the

The first P, Preparation, equips us with the right knowledge to put us in charge of our own career destination and helps us begin to develop a roadmap to get there.

achievements to which we aspire, and the right timing and language to articulate them. We want to determine the direction of our paths rather than allowing someone else to do so and being an observer. This enables us to gain a greater sense of control over our own journey and destiny. The first P, Preparation, equips us with the right knowledge to put us in charge of our own career destination and helps us begin to develop a roadmap to get there.

It is crucial that you know your strengths as well as your limitations, interests, values, priorities and goals. Be well versed in your own achievements and accomplishments. Storytelling is the best way to communicate results and of holding your audience's attention. The key is to clearly distinguish yourself from your colleagues, highlighting the differentiating factors you possess and offer. Have a crisp and clear message when articulating and communicating your expertise. Keep it simple and easy to understand. Be goal-oriented, and have a mission for yourself with specific short- and long-term goals and objectives. Reassess and update your goals regularly with a concise plan, and stay true to yourself! As a result, you will come across as confident, focused, purposeful and self-directed.

When I started my coaching and consulting business, I had a list of bullets regarding my experiences and credentials that I felt differentiated me in my field, such as: over 25 years' human resources experience working with professionals across all industries and professions; an extensive network and strong affiliations within the business and human resource communities; a unique mix of business knowledge and "real world" experience; a core competency of relationship building; and customized services to meet the needs of each client. Even so, when I emphasized these differentiated factors, they didn't feel or sound compelling enough. Were these truly the reasons why my clients engaged me instead of a competitor? When I asked myself this question, I was not confident in the answer. So in my third year of business, I decided to go right to my clients and ask them this specific question to uncover the actual reasons they engaged my services.

After reaching out to several clients, what I learned is that regardless of the industry or size of the organization, the two common themes that stood out were my style and reputation.

It all came together for me! Relationship-building has always been one of my strengths and has played a major role in my success throughout all phases of my career. Now, it was all clear to me – it would make sense, therefore, that my differentiating factors had more to do with who I was, my approach, my credibility, what I offered, and how I dealt with my clients rather than my bulleted list of my experiences. This allowed me to tell my stories with authenticity that truly reflected my value as a results-oriented, relationship-driven, authentic, credible, and high-quality consultant. Therefore, I started to change my messaging to reflect these differentiators, using them as a springboard which enabled me to tell a story or two focused on specific results. It shouldn't surprise you that in doing so, my message is delivered with much more ease, fluency and effectiveness!

In fact, one of my clients allowed me to use a direct quote on the welcome page of my website that says it for me:

Clients engage Rita Allen because of her unique **style** and her **reputation**. Her style is a strong, totally approachable leader: sincere, authentic and credible. Her outstanding reputation in the marketplace is simply a reflection of her ability to deliver superb service and consistently excellent outcomes for her clients.

~ **CYNTHIA M. CONNELLY**
FORMER VP MARKETING
ENCORE ETC., INC.(RETAIL CONSUMER SERVICES COMPANY)

Telling your story that focuses on your differentiators starts with much discovery and exploration. Once you are able to peel away all the layers of your past successes and challenges and get to your core, you will have a clear sense of purpose and the groundwork for packaging and presenting your personal brand.

Establishing and building a strong network is also essential. We do not build successful careers on an island. Having a solid network of trusted colleagues provides us with resources, connections, feedback and support that are vital for enhancing our knowledge and experiences. Let me illustrate this point with a personal example. When I established my business, it was largely due to my existing network that I was able to secure referrals and generate new leads. Without those contacts, it would have been much more difficult to get my business off the ground. Think of it as planting a garden – once you plant the seeds, you have to nourish the garden with water, sunshine, and food as well as by trimming and weeding the garden on a regular, ongoing basis for the flowers to blossom. Relationships require the same care and nurturing to flourish and grow, so invest in maintaining and nurturing long-lasting relationships with your contacts.

Last but not least you, and only you, are in charge of your attitude. Believe it or not, positive attitude and a sense of humor are most important in setting a strong foundation for a successful marketing strategy. I have learned the most profound and lasting lessons from my mistakes rather than my successes. It takes a great deal of confidence and comfort in ourselves to get to this point, but once we learn to see the cup half full and expect some bumps along the way to our goals, it truly makes the journey a lot more fun, enlightening and exhilarating. As Charles Swindoll says, "I am convinced that life is 10% what happens to me and 90% how I react to it... and so it is with you... we are in charge of our Attitudes." [3]

---

3   Swindoll, Charles R. (1995). *Attitudes: The Power of a Positive Outlook.* Grand Rapids: Zondervan: p. 1951

Self Assessment

The first step in Preparation is self assessment. There are many tools, surveys and exercises to help you with your self assessment process: hundreds and hundreds of options that are formal ways of discovering more about your personality, preferences, learning style, skills, motivation, energy, interests, etc. It is important to identify those that are most appropriate for you and will provide the specific type of information you are seeking. Every individual is different and may prefer to explore certain areas more than others which will help to determine the most relevant assessments. In the end, the objective is to learn as much as you can about yourself, not leaving any stone unturned to reflect in an intimate and honest manner. The areas to explore are:

- **Strengths and Areas for Development**

- **Competencies Required and Competencies Possessed**

- **Interests: Personal and Professional**

- **Values and Priorities**

- **Goals and Aspirations: Short- and Long-Term**

Keeping a journal is an excellent way to reflect over an extended period of time and keep track of your likes, dislikes, strengths, limitations, weaknesses, interests and aspirations. As you do so, you will begin to see patterns emerge that are quite revealing. Jot down things that appeal to you, tasks that are energizing or draining, untapped or overused skills. This is a time for deep self-exploration, and you will be surprised at what you discover! Your findings can be logged in a Personal SWOT (Strengths, Weaknesses, Opportunities, and Threats) Analysis to truly understand and leverage your worth and value-add. (More on this on page 23.)

Throughout this book, I will be sprinkling in real stories of some of my past clients who achieved this level of self discovery and were able to identify, build and enhance their personal brand. These stories will be brought to you in their own words allowing them to share their experience and journey. You will be inspired and encouraged by their stories. I know I was! Here is the first.

Meet Charlie Anderson, Independent Consultant:

As a human resources professional in my mid-sixties I found myself floundering about in terms of finding my next job. At my age, I didn't want to keep doing the same old thing. I have also come to terms with my inability to tolerate bureaucracy or to take a job where I wouldn't be fully utilized. Rita asked me a number of hard questions – What do you love to do at work? What do you do best? How do others see you? After you define what you want, how are you going to get it? Answering these questions and others, taking assessments, and really thinking about the future allowed me to move forward in a more positive direction.

I am a typical "Baby Boomer." Like others of my generation I am not interested in retiring and sitting on a rocker on the front porch. I want to continue contributing to organizations, develop others who want to manage and contribute to those less fortunate. Our definition of retirement is different from our parents. Most of us will not get pensions, many of us have worked long workweeks of 50-60 hours most of our lives and don't know how to just stop. The thought of retirement scares many of us. We may be financially secure, although that is not the majority position, but what will we do with our time?

Taking the time to reflect and explore to find the answers to these difficult questions helped me look at who I am through thoughtful questioning. These were questions I should have asked myself but avoided, including the most basic questions: Who am I and what do I want to be?

We then analyzed data to fine tune the responses. The assessments helped me better understand where I am in terms of organizational development.

Next I sought out and received anonymous feedback from former coworkers, family and friends to gain insight from others who knew me and worked with me. They addressed my strengths, my qualities, my areas for development as well as offered perspective on how I am perceived by others. The results of this activity were incredibly powerful. I learned that what I did and how I did it were inseparable from what people thought I was as a person. I should not have been surprised that who I am inside and outside of work is the same. Funny, I thought I operated differently in my different roles. This continuity of behavior allowed me to see that my work life and my real life overlapped and matched. This realization gave me a clarity that had been missing.

I then made a list of the things I liked to do, the kinds of colleagues I enjoyed, and a work life that did not exclude my personal life. This empowered me to screen through numerous opportunities that surfaced through networking. My confidence in my knowledge allowed others to see a "fit" or not. People who met me saw the real person with all the baggage that accompanies it. My clarity in what I wanted to do demonstrates to others that I wanted a role that could make significant contributions to the organization but that I wasn't concerned about title, money or status. Since this discovery I have been presented with many opportunities to join companies. I have decided to focus on contract work at present coupled with the desire to know and positively influence my five grandchildren. I have never felt freer or more energized. I have also come to the conclusion that I am a Generation Y in a Baby Boomer's body. I hope to never stop doing the things I love.

STAYING TRUE TO VALUES

A critical part of the self-assessment process is identifying our values, those areas that are most important to us, and then prioritizing them. Awareness of our values should be a guide to many of our decisions throughout our career and life. Often, when someone is struggling with a specific situation or individual, the core of the issue tends to come back to a compromise of values.

When we seek a new job and/ or other types of opportunities, our values should be front and center in assessing the fit of that possibility. Are the values of the  environment, company, team, leader and/or within your individual role aligned with your own? Sometimes, they will be completely aligned, and other times they may be somewhat aligned or not aligned at all. In those scenarios, understanding what you will be compromising and how much you will be sacrificing will be a critical decision factor.

Values are so important, and yet when you ask someone to tell you their top five values, many folks cannot clearly answer that question. These are the areas of most importance to us, the vital foundation and critical drivers of our happiness. More often than not, when a person begins to lose interest or is disengaged, it is due to a lack of alignment of values within the company culture, team culture, with their leader/manager, and/or within their individual role. Knowing your values alerts you to when there is a lack of alignment, and that knowledge prepares you to weigh the respective benefits of compromising that value for the benefit of gaining a reward, or of making the difficult decision to move elsewhere.

Are the values of the environment, company, team, leader and/or individual role aligned with your own? Sometimes, they will be completely aligned, and other times they may be somewhat aligned or not aligned at all. In those scenarios, understanding what you will be compromising and how much you will be sacrificing will be a critical decision factor.

Change is the only constant we can expect every day. It is unrealistic to expect all our values to be 100% aligned all of the time. Tomorrow your company could be acquired, your position could be altered, or you could have a new manager. Therefore, it is important to keep an open mind and be flexible. However, when we know our values thoroughly, we can understand where compromise is feasible, and appreciate what we will gain in return. After spending a good deal of time assessing our strengths, areas of development, limitations, interests, values and aspirations, we can start planning how we might leverage those strengths while addressing some of our weaknesses.

As mentioned on page 18, a *personal SWOT analysis* is an ideal exercise for organizing and condensing your self-assessment . A SWOT analysis is a thorough examination of your strengths (areas which you excel), weaknesses (areas for development), opportunities (to be seized for development) and threats (potential challenges and obstacles). Through this process, you can strategize ways to leverage your strengths to take advantage of opportunities, address weaknesses and minimize threats. Once you do so, you can create an *action plan* with specific steps for moving forward and keeping yourself accountable.

Use the following worksheets to assess your values, conduct your personal SWOT analysis, and create your action plan.

VALUES AND PRIORITIES

Rank the following values according to the priority you place on it from 1 to 20 (one being the highest priority) based on your personal assessment:

Recognition ....

Achievement ....

Autonomy ....

Wealth ....

Health ....

Integrity ....

Balance ....

Loyalty ....

Control ....

Competitiveness ....

Creativity ....

Power ....

Cooperation ....

Collaboration ....

Challenge ....

Respect ....

Personal Growth and Advancement ....

Efficiency ....

Spirituality ....

Security ....

Responsibility ....

Education/Knowledge ....

Fun ....

Inner Peace ....

Acceptance ....

Self-Actualization ....

Family ....

Add in others of your own: _____

_____

_____

_____

SWOT ANALYSIS[4]	Key Strengths:	Critical Weaknesses:
Key Opportunities:	Strategies for using strengths to take advantage of opportunities...	Strategies for addressing weaknesses to take advantage of opportunities...
Critical Threats:	Strategies for using strengths to avoid threats or turn threats into opportunities...	Strategies for addressing weaknesses to avoid threats...

4   Source: Northeastern University, "Developing The Strategic Leader."
Instructor: Lynne C. Levesque, Ed.D.

ACTION PLAN

Developing and Executing an Action Plan

A) Identify development areas you'd like to address and prioritize.

_____

_____

_____

_____

B) Spell out realistic steps to achieve success with specific tasks, and action items.

_____

_____

_____

_____

C) Plan out a timeline you will follow and for which you will be accountable.

_____

_____

_____

_____

D) Create a follow up strategy to measure and evaluate your success. Make adjustments as needed.

_____

_____

_____

_____

RITA B. ALLEN ASSOCIATES
Career Management Strategies for Individuals and Organizations

Value-Add & Differentiators

If you could use one word to describe yourself, what would it be? If you could use one word how others would describe you, what would it be?

- Are the words the same or different?
- Why do you think this is?
- How do you stand out amongst your peers and colleagues?
- What makes you YOU?

Whenever I ask people the last question, it seems to create a lot of angst and hesitation. People tend either to focus solely on their skills, abilities and achievements, or they believe that there needs to be something intrinsically extraordinary about them that suggests standout performance. In some cases, individuals do have a clear niche or unique skill that others do not possess. In many cases, however, we may have similar skills to our peers… but what makes us who we are is always unique! Most of the time our personal brand is more about our style, our approach, our personality, and/or the stamp we leave behind. Sometimes we can be our own worst critics, or take a lot for granted. We are not always aware of the mark we can and do leave on our work and on others.

Our most important revelation may be discovering how we differentiate ourselves and stand apart from others: this is what truly makes us who we are.

Meet Pattie Manning, Human Resources Professional:

After almost two years of being unemployed from a wonderful role as Human Resource Director in a biotechnology company, I was pretty much at the end of being able to muster any self-confidence as I was continuing to search for a job. Throughout that period, my resume seemed to be getting me interviews but I either wasn't getting past the first round or if I did, I was consistently coming in second. I was working as a consultant in a small company for a CEO I had worked for in the past, but the role was small and not very challenging, which also didn't help boost my ego. Here I was, a career human resources generalist who had been a Director for over 15 years, and I couldn't land a job.

When Rita suggested a Personal Branding session, I thought it was time for me to do a bit more work on myself, my view of what I was and wanted to be known for, and a self-analysis of what I was doing wrong in all of these interviews. I felt like that session was a huge turning point for me. The people in the room were feeling somewhat the same, most of them searching for how to market themselves in a job search. We had all used all the buzzwords, all the tools, all the right avenues, but still something was missing.

For me that session was a light bulb going on in my head! I was able to speak in that group and feel confident that I wasn't being judged. Everyone had their story and the exercises brought out experiences to be valued. I struggled with some of the thought process, but stopped thinking at one point and realized that it was safe to just be who I was, and that my voice had value.

When we thought about our own brand, it dawned on me that I do have a brand… my own brand of Human Resources to bring to a company. I'm not like other Human Resource people. My past is different, my style is different and my creativity is in the way I handle problems. The big moment there for me was when we had to say what sets us apart and makes our individual brand. Only two words would come to mind and I waited until everyone else had shared their thoughts. Then there it was – my two words just came out. I am a blend of experience and personality. That's what makes my brand. From that day on I always had that in my mind as I presented myself in interviews as well as in my next role. I had confidence and faith and was able to build on that foundation. I truly believe the process and steps we engaged in during that session woke me up and gave me the confidence I needed to move on.

I guess what changed for me was I finally became comfortable with my own brand and what I really had to bring to the party. I went into the last round of interviews with more confidence and started to look at what that opportunity would mean for me. For example, I had two companies at the same time where I was in the advanced round of interviews. With one of the companies I had met with the new CEO and he asked me why I didn't have a degree in Human Resources. That threw me off a little, but my response was that my experience more than covered what a degree would have provided. At this point in my career, I had more to offer than someone coming out of school or someone with only a few years of experience. I was able to provide examples of strategic involvement in each of the companies I worked and success with creating, building or changing a culture. That meant understanding business and people, management and employees. That's who I am and what I do.

That company called me back again and when I went back for the final round -- I felt like I was interviewing them. The feeling was amazing. I believed in myself and what I had to offer. I had my story and didn't apologize for it the way I had in the past. That wasn't the position I eventually took but it helped me negotiate with the company for the position I did accept.

I love my job, my company and my coworkers. I have come to this role with the ability to believe in what I know and it has certainly paid off for me in the role I get to play here. I'm a manager, coach, referee, cheerleader and team member and consistently balance those roles every day. I have never worked harder in a job nor been happier to be where I am.

I have been able to pass along how important it is to go into a job search with a full understanding of who you are, what you do and the value you offer to your organization.

The preparation process requires a deep intimacy with ourselves and understanding of who we are and what we are all about. Self-awareness is very difficult and not a process we do once and stop. It requires on-going exploration and awareness. We need to be open to:

- **Continuous learning about ourselves and what makes us tick.**

- **Performing a regular inventory of all our skills, competencies, knowledge and abilities.**

- Recognizing our strengths as well as our limitations.

- Staying fluent and well versed in what we have achieved, our interests and our aspirations.

- Defining the unique characteristics, traits and/or experiences we have to offer that set us apart.

- Owning the choices we have made.

- Being able to articulate them, telling "our story" with pride and confidence.

What are our areas of functional and/or technical expertise? Have we established specific niches for which we are sought after and well known? How do we differentiate ourselves from our peers and colleagues? Keeping it simple and easy to understand will greatly assist in creating a crisp, clear message when articulating and communicating our personal brand.

All of us have different ways of thinking through these questions and getting them on paper. I find it helpful to keep a journal where I bullet my thoughts and reflections. Others may find it more comfortable to use a smartphone or tablet, or create a spreadsheet. The key is to process and track this information in a way that works for you. Be creative and get inspired to make it yours. Let me share an example of another client who created a visual graphic that allowed her to chart her competencies as follows:

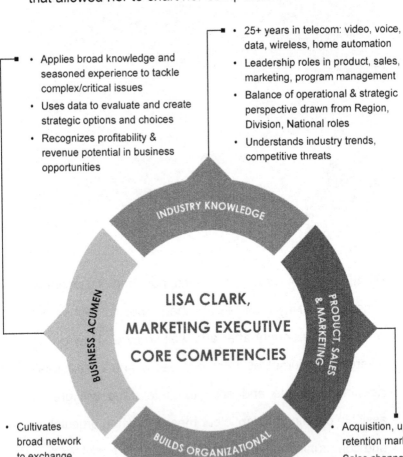

- Applies broad knowledge and seasoned experience to tackle complex/critical issues
- Uses data to evaluate and create strategic options and choices
- Recognizes profitability & revenue potential in business opportunities

- 25+ years in telecom: video, voice, data, wireless, home automation
- Leadership roles in product, sales, marketing, program management
- Balance of operational & strategic perspective drawn from Region, Division, National roles
- Understands industry trends, competitive threats

INDUSTRY KNOWLEDGE

BUSINESS ACUMEN

LISA CLARK, MARKETING EXECUTIVE CORE COMPETENCIES

PRODUCT, SALES & MARKETING

BUILDS ORGANIZATIONAL KNOWLEDGE

- Cultivates broad network to exchange ideas & rally support for the mission
- Navigate org & functional boundaries to shape stakeholder opinions
- Collaborative style inspires trust
- Extensive cross-functional leadership
- Managed team of 15; skilled mentor

- Acquisition, upgrade, retention marketing
- Sales channel management
- Product management
- Program management of initiatives driving higher share, revenue, cost savings
- Competitive thought leader

360-DEGREE FEEDBACK

Even the most honest and searching self assessment may not fully reveal what we need to know. We may not always be as objective as others in recognizing our development needs, as well as our strengths. That is why it's just as important to ask others for input to confirm self-perception and uncover blind spots. Engage your managers, peers, colleagues, staff members, clients, vendors, other stakeholders, as well as friends and family for their feedback. Asking for details and examples can also help to develop a more rounded picture. Select participants who will provide honest, valuable and constructive insights from a variety of perspectives.

Remember, there can be times when our intent does not align with impact and having honest feedback will provide valuable lessons for our own development.

It's important to maintain a good attitude and sense of humor, even if some of the feedback you receive is hard to accept. Be open to receiving feedback and stay focused on your ultimate objective of personal and professional development. Keep in mind that receiving feedback can be jolting at times for all of us, and don't allow the discomfort to be a barrier. Try not to rationalize, be defensive, or qualify your behaviors. Embrace feedback as the true perceptions of those providing it. Take it all in and accept that is coming from a place of support and growth. Remember, there can be times when our intent does not align with impact and having honest feedback will provide valuable lessons for our own development. Focus on your strengths and leverage them to enhance areas needing further development. Keep an open dialogue as you move forward encouraging additional feedback on a regular basis. Most importantly, be sure to thank everyone who participated.

We wear different hats at work, home and at play, so it's important to ask a wide variety of contacts for feedback. This is referred to as a 360-degree feedback process. Many individuals and organizations use "360s" to gain deeper and more objective assessments of capabilities and career highlights. There are many formal 360 feedback assessment tools available that you could use to collect anonymous feedback from others. You can also follow these four simple steps:

1. **Think of four to five people** you can reach out to that represent a mix of your managers, colleagues, peers, colleagues, staff, friends and family. Be sure to have a mix from each category and select those that you know will be honest, objective, constructive and insightful.

2. **Contact these individuals.** Explain your exploration process, how much you would value their input, and the important role they would be playing by participating in this 360 feedback exercise.

3. **Once you have their commitment and agreement** to take part, ask them to provide you with honest feedback in writing on the questions below. (Many no- or low-cost Web survey tools are available to ease the process for contributors and to gather feedback anonymously, encouraging more frank and constructive commentary.)

   • What do you see as my strengths – my strongest abilities and competencies?

   • What are my areas for development?

   • How would you describe me, my style and approach? How am I perceived by others?

4. **Collect feedback from all** and take time to reflect on all of the different perspectives and begin to incorporate them into your self-assessment process.

IDENTIFYING DIFFERENTIATORS

After collecting feedback from others and incorporating it into our own self assessment, we can begin to identify our differentiators. The next step is to take stock of all our accomplishments throughout our career, from day one in our first job to the current day. Ideally we have kept track of our achievements in some way, but if we have not, it is not too late.

Compile a running list of everything you have been a part of accomplishing in all of your jobs. You can create various categories of your field that I call "buckets," and then create a list of bullet items for all that you have accomplished in each of those buckets. It can be a cheat sheet of sorts: a reminder of all that you have achieved. Of course this takes a long time to prepare, and requires a lot of reflection, research and recollection, but you cannot afford not to complete this process. Refer to performance reviews, old resumes, old job descriptions, testimonials, references, project reports, and any other history of your track record that will enable you to be fully knowledgeable and informed about your accomplishments. Through this process, you can discover what was your proudest accomplishment, which was most difficult, most challenging, most rewarding, and so on.

It will also give you an opportunity to incorporate your differentiators into your accomplishments and to frame these accomplishments with results achieved, by way of storytelling. As we discussed earlier, the best way to illustrate your results is through a story.

STORYTELLING

Storytelling is the most compelling way to communicate an event: specifically, its results or impact. Whenever I conduct presentations or workshops, I always use storytelling as a way to get my point across — and inevitably the moment I begin a story, you can hear a pin drop in the room. It's a sure way to get and keep people's attention rather than citing a multitude of facts, figures and details. Think of the people you listen to more readily. Are they able to capture your undivided attention due to the storytelling nature of their communications?

Whether you are a leader trying to inspire and motivate others or a professional at any level aspiring to pursue your goals within or outside of your organization, the best way to influence others and talk about your accomplishments is through storytelling. The key is in capturing the essence of any event and turning it into a story. We may think of it as an art but in reality, there are three easy steps to crafting and communicating your story.

THREE EASY STEPS OF STORYTELLING

1. Describe the situation: set the stage by identifying the issue at hand.

2. Actions taken: outline the specific actions you took to address the issue.

3. Results: explain the ultimate impact and outcomes achieved.

We all want to make a difference in our careers not only by communicating more effectively, but by influencing others in a way that yields results. Practicing storytelling allows us to emphasize our contributions while engaging others to follow our lead. Articulating your vision, strategy and actions by way of stories is memorable and allows your listeners to be able to truly relate to you more effectively and intimately.

Crafting your story is half the equation. The other half is delivering your story. Do you speak or write with passion, enthusiasm and animation? If you've ever heard, "It wasn't what you said, but how you said it," you intuitively recognize the importance of delivery.

One of my favorite successful entrepreneurs is Barbara Corcoran, a real estate guru in New York City who is also an author, television personality and motivational speaker. One of the books she has written (with Bruce Littlefield), *Use What You've Got...& Other Business Lessons I Learned from My Mom*, exemplifies the art of communicating through storytelling. She offers what amounts to a sales manual through life lessons she learned growing up in a family with ten children![4] It's humorous, memorable and robust – an easy read that leaves you with effective tools, strategies and tips.

Some of the most successful leaders have left their mark with their stories. They may have created and built successful companies, discovered cures for diseases, led our country during difficult times, or brought joy and happiness into the lives of others. When we remember incredible people who have influenced others and/or accomplished great things, we often think of their legacies in terms of their stories: the situation at hand, actions they

When we remember incredible people who have influenced others and/or accomplished great things, we often think of their legacies in terms of their stories: the situation at hand, actions they took, and results they achieved.

---

4   Corcoran, Barbara and Littlefield, Bruce (2003). *Use What You've Got, and Other Business Lessons I Learned from My Mom*. New York: Penguin.

took, and results they achieved. Every day, at work, home or play, we encounter and experience stories on greater or lesser scales. How well do we communicate when we relay the events of our day to others? The truth is that we don't have to wait until we leave our legacy to tell great stories. Every day we have opportunities to share our challenges, accomplishments, and lessons learned. Anyone who has children appreciates how effective it is when you try to make a point to your kids through your own childhood stories, such as a tale about a difficult experience or a bad choice. This is always more impactful than preaching dos and don'ts to them. The same can be said about the workplace. We will be more successful communicating with our colleagues, clients, peers, team members and managers when we articulate our message via storytelling. Practicing this skill will strengthen our ability to influence others and leave lasting positive impressions.

Most importantly, a story is only effective when it is delivered **with authenticity**. Keep it real, be sincere and genuine in order to build and earn trust! Our ability to craft our stories will allow us to effectively discuss how we add value, showcasing our personal brand and not just saying what our differentiators are but actually illustrating what they are through the results and outcomes we have achieved, with ease, sincerity and authenticity.

Goals

The self-assessment process required us to define what we have to offer so that we know our value-add. The next practice, of discovering what we want, requires us to identify specific short-term and long-term goals as well as an execution plan we are ready to articulate and discuss.

Every December or January, many of us reflect on the previous year and think of ways to start fresh. We consider new approaches with great intention. Some of us write down these thoughts, some create mental checklists, and some do neither forgetting all about them within weeks. A number of years ago, I made a commitment to block out three hours the first Friday of every December dedicated to planning and setting my goals for the following year in addition to revisiting the previous year, reviewing, reevaluating and adjusting as necessary. This allows me to start the new year with focus and determination. In addition, I create timelines throughout the year for me to check in and see how well I am progressing towards accomplishing these goals. Since doing so, I have actually achieved my goals each year and have done so in a timely and effective manner.

Our goals can only be reached through a vehicle of a plan, in which we must fervently believe, and upon which we must vigorously act. There is no other route to success.

~ **PABLO PICASSO**
PAINTER, SCULPTOR, POET, AND PLAYWRIGHT

Similarly, we all need to have **a mission for our career and specific goals we want to accomplish.** Without a plan, we do not have direction or criteria for accountability. If you reflect on last year, were there missed opportunities as a result of not having set goals for the year? Did you hold back your career by not identifying specific goals that you wrote down and reviewed monthly for progress? Annual goal setting will allow you to achieve the following outcomes:

- A mission for your career

- Specific goals you want to accomplish both personally and professionally

- Plans, with detailed directions for execution

- Criteria for accountability

The following **five-step process** can help you stay on target and achieve the kind of success you envision for yourself. It will enable you to move your career in alignment with your aspirations, while remaining open to unexpected opportunities and exploring new paths and directions.

Step 1: Identify Vision, Mission and Values

- **Vision:** What do you envision for yourself, currently and in the future?

- **Mission:** What is the purpose of your career for you, as it exists and ideally?

- **Core Values:** What matters most to you? Identify your top five values.

Step 2: Create "SMART" Goals[5] That Are...

- **S**pecific: precise, focused, and well-defined, not vague

- **M**easurable: defined by appropriate metrics to qualify and quantify success

- **A**ttainable: reachable, appropriate, and achievable

- **R**ealistic/Relevant: results-oriented and rewarding

- **T**ime-Bound: having specific, trackable target dates for completion

---

5   Cunningham, James, George Doran and Arthur Miller. "There's a S.M.A.R.T. way to write management's goals and objectives." *Management Review* November 1981: Vol. 70, Issue 11.

Step 3: Develop Goal Setting Process

- **Short-Term Goals:** Determine short term expectations that will allow you to achieve your objectives for the next one to three years, while laying the groundwork and steps to achieve your longer term hopes for the future. What are the short term goals you want and need to achieve?

- **Long-Term Goals:** As you have defined the mission and purpose of your career, determine what your long-term aspirations are, looking ahead at least over the next three to five years with specific goals that are aligned with your mission, vision and desires. We need to know what direction we are headed so that everything we do, both short- and long-term, allows us to accomplish our vision and reach our destination. Start with the long-term picture and then work on planning when and how you will arrive there.

- **Realistic Obstacles and Challenges That May Be Encountered:** Whenever we travel on a journey, we want to plan ahead and be proactive, anticipating barriers, obstacles and challenges that may arise so as to be prepared to handle them in an objective manner. First identify what these challenges and obstacles may be, and develop strategies to minimize and/or deal with them.

- **Execution Strategy:** Create a road map for achieving these goals by identifying exactly what, how and when you will reach your destination and fulfill your goals. This requires much planning, discipline and commitment as well as the confidence and initiative to engage the support and help of others as necessary. Having a precise and detailed plan will ensure success and goal accomplishment.

- **Follow-Up Plan to Review and Evaluate Your Progress:** Establish a formalized plan to assess your ability to stay the course. Evaluate where you are in your goal accomplishment as well as the continued relevance of your goals, and do so at the very least on a monthly basis, if not more frequently, making adjustments as needed. Keep and stay accountable for your results.

Step 4: Determine Commitment

- Write down personal and professional goals – put them on paper.

- Reach out to others for help and support.

- Earn trust and gain cooperation from others involved.

- Commit to staying focused – make and keep yourself a priority.

- Live a more intentional life, with purpose and clarity.

Step 5: Maintain Accountability

Accountability is a critical piece of the overall goal setting process because in the end, it's all about staying true to ourselves, being disciplined and following our dreams. Working within a system that is comfortable and doable for us, rather than creating something we dread doing and avoid, will ensure that we stay on track. We want to look forward to this and embrace it!

- **Revisit, reassess and reevaluate goals** on a regular basis.

- **Make adjustments as appropriate and necessary**, keeping an open mind and being flexible.

- **Continue to formulate an approach to setting your personal and professional goals** that will work best for you. Make it your own; create a formula that is best aligned with your needs and style. For example, I like to condense my goals onto an index card and carry it in my bag to easily reference on a monthly basis. Someone else may prefer to have an informal log on their iPhone, or a reminder in Outlook. Find what you prefer and work it.

One of the most striking findings of Gail Matthews' Dominican University study, which I touched on on page 6, was the degree to which subjects who wrote down their goals succeeded in accomplishing them versus those who did not:

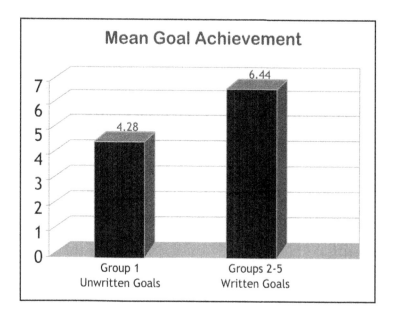

Clearly, the act of writing down their goals helped to keep Groups 2-5 accountable to achieve their goals.[6]

6   Ibid: p. 6

Meet Dan Kraus, Entrepreneur:

I'd worked in larger technology companies – mostly software companies – for 20 years. During the dot-bomb bust, I'd taken a run at running a consulting firm with a couple of partners, and one by myself as well. Neither were particularly successful. In 2009, after a pretty successful run at one of the largest software companies in the world, I was trying to figure out what I wanted to do next.

This journey of figuring out what Simon Sinek most elegantly calls "Your Why" wasn't too long or arduous. It came down to three parts:

1. What do I do everyday

2. What do I know that I think I am an expert in

3. What do people need that they will pay money for[7]

Then it was figuring out how to get these all together in a company and get myself going. So step one was looking at what I do every day, and what I have done every day over my career, and breaking it down. I needed to clearly understand, for me, what I actually did; and which parts I liked and what I hated. I obviously wanted to do more of what I liked and less of what I didn't. This discovery led me to make the statement I still say today – that I am corporately unemployable – because I really dislike the "palace intrigue" of corporate politics.

---

7   Sinek, Simon (2009). *Start with Why: How Great Leaders Inspire Everyone to Take Action.* New York: Penguin

One of the things that I did uncover in this exercise was how much I truly enjoyed learning new things and trying to invent a better way of doing things with new knowledge.

Then I needed to figure out what I was an expert in. With 20 years of technology sales and marketing in my background, it wasn't too hard. I really understand the challenges in this complex buying process, and I had real empathy for the customer who had to navigate it. I also realized that I clearly understood the consultant's point of view as they stood between the software publisher/hardware developer and the customer that had to use the products.

What finally crystallized my business for me was when I thought back through the experiences of the last few years. When I looked at the problems I consistently saw, that no one was solving well, what came to me was a statement one of the software dealers had made. He had commented that he was sick of wasting money on marketing; they had just spent $30,000 on a radio campaign and got nothing from it.

That was it! I'd build a company that helped small tech firms stop wasting money on marketing. We'd help them do it right and if need be, do it for them...and in four and a half years, we've gone from just me to five full time and two part time folks. We've worked with hundreds of clients. We are learning new things every day. We are having fun and there are no politics.

The process of truly understanding what I valued, what I did well and what I wanted led me to discoveries that played to the areas I was passionate about while staying true to what mattered most to me!

GOALS ARE THE PATHWAY TO SUCCESS

Remember the three practices that successful professionals share?

THREE COMMONALITIES OF SUCCESSFUL PROFESSIONALS

1.   Know what they have to offer (Their value-add)

2.   Know what they want (Have specific goals)

3.   Know how to ask for it (Advocate effectively)

How would you answer this question: *"If I could offer you your ideal job (or project) on a silver platter tomorrow, what would that be?"* This is another question that many people find hard to answer without having taken the time to set specific short- and long-term goals and objectives that they reassess and update regularly.

If you have a plan and stay true to yourself, the result will assure that when you tell your story, you come across as confident, focused, purposeful and self-directed.

Establishing our goals is an effective way to clarify our vision and set the stage for success, but it takes resilience and commitment. We know that successful organizations strive to attract the right mix of talent, develop them and keep them engaged to fulfill their business goals and objectives. By knowing our own goals, we can ensure alignment with organizational and functional goals.

Accountability is a critical piece of the overall goal setting process because in the end, it's all about staying true to ourselves, being disciplined and following our dreams. Working within a system that is comfortable and doable for us, rather than creating something we dread doing and avoid, will ensure that we stay on track.

Enjoy the process, set yourself apart and push yourself out of your comfort zone as you kick off every year! Use the following worksheet to assess and determine your goals.

GOALS ASSESSMENT

1. Define overall mission and objective for your career:

_____

_____

_____

_____

_____

2. Long-term aspirations:

_____

_____

_____

_____

_____

3. Short-term expectations:

_____

_____

_____

_____

_____

4. Realistic obstacles and challenges:

_____

_____

_____

_____

_____

5. Goal Setting

    a. Short-term goals: 1 to 3 years:

    _____

    _____

    _____

    _____

    b. Long-term goals: 5+ years

    _____

    _____

    _____

    _____

6. Execution Strategy:

    _____

    _____

    _____

    _____

7. Follow-Up Plan:

    _____

    _____

    _____

    _____

    _____

    _____

    _____

RITA B. ALLEN ASSOCIATES
Career Management Strategies for Individuals and Organizations

Network

Like it or not, the ability to network effectively and consistently remains one of the key ingredients in managing a successful career.

Regardless of your field, industry, level or geography, it is essential to embrace networking, get comfortable with it, and truly develop the "art of networking." I call it an art because every individual will make it their own and create a landscape that is unique and appropriate for them. We could even replace "networking" with the term "relationship building." Think of it as having meaningful conversations and building productive connections, with the goal of establishing, creating, and nurturing strong long-lasting relationships through many venues. It's just as much about giving back and being a resource to others as it is about gaining support. Actually, it's even better to approach it as a way of focusing on other people's needs and interests. Part of our personal brand is correlated to the kind of network we establish and how effectively we build and nurture these relationships.

Networking includes internal networking within your organization as well as external networking within your industry and field. Both are equally vital for career success and should be embarked upon with different plans while playing off of the other. Always look to enhance your connections and relationships within your organization. This means within your team, department, function, region, and beyond. It is equally important to identify contacts outside of your functional area and tap into those colleagues you don't work with regularly but should know and be a resource to each other. Having a strong mix of efforts around internal and external networking is key.

Many people still believe that relationship building is most critical when they decide to embark on a new job search, and of course it is important at that time. In fact, there have been many surveys over the last decade indicating the relevance of networking as a top source for finding a job. However, don't make the mistake of thinking that's the only time. While networking remains the top source for learning about new job opportunities, it is also the top source for business development, resource referrals, vendor selection, market data, and industry trends, as well as a source of relevant information for your business and personal career.

I was one of those people who did not quite understand the link between networking and successful career management early in my career. I certainly knew it was important, but did not see it as a strategic imperative that played a major role in my personal and professional development.

During one of my job transitions, I started to connect the dots and see that networking not only helped me with that job search, but established connections that were the start of something much bigger! I started to see the formation of relationships that were ongoing, productive and mutually meaningful. I also started to see how those connections generated new connections, resulting in even deeper knowledge and resources for me as a human resources professional.

Once I then made the transition to the search business, my appreciation for the power of true relationship building was a key ingredient in my success as an executive search consultant. After 16 years in search and building a very strong network of trusted colleagues, clients, supporters and friends, starting my own business was a natural progression for me. My network was a solid foundation that allowed me to do so in a way that was seamless and empowering. Having such a strong and interconnected group of supporters, colleagues, advisors, and friends made all the difference. It also enabled me to be successful throughout my career to the point that I grew to recognize it as one of my differentiators: a way that I stand out within my field and industry. Not only do I appreciate the importance of my network, I invest in nurturing and enhancing my relationships, giving them the high level of time and priority that reflects their value to me.

Let me share some tried and true tips for building your network and engaging in successful networking strategies. I learned these many years ago from one of my mentors, **Bob Gatti**, and they remain as compelling and relevant today.

TEN TIPS FOR SUCCESSFUL NETWORKING

1. Identify specific target markets. Focus on influential people within your field that you should meet and begin the process of building and nurturing relationships with them. Identify the segments of your market where your focus will reap the most rewards. You may decide to break your target relationships down by level, specialty, geography, industry and/or a variety of other factors. The important thing is to have a plan – begin to narrow down to two to three specific target areas to get you off the starting block. You need a starting point that is specific, focused and attainable. If you aim too broadly, you will likely be ineffective and not get the maximum reward out of your efforts. A broad target will minimize your reach and increase your risk of not penetrating your target segment(s). Avoid throwing a wide net and not capturing the right level of depth. Focus on specific targets to build quality relationships.

2. **Know your marketplace.** Be well-read. Stay on top of current practices, trends, new businesses and resources. Join professional associations and attend meetings, seminars, conferences, and networking events where you can stay educated on the most recent developments and challenges. This is also where you will continue to meet people of influence within your field, putting the right types of resources at your fingertips. Read appropriate trade journals, periodicals, newspapers, and websites that make you aware of up-to-the-minute changes. This will also keep you on top of your competition and lower your risk of encountering any surprises.

3. **Be visible and "in play."** Put yourself in a position to meet people. Networking internally within your organization is critical, but it is only one part of the equation. Take an active role within your professional and personal community. Many people make the mistake of devoting all of their time and effort to putting their heads down and doing their jobs. I've heard many people say "I don't have any time to get out and network." The truth is that you have to discipline yourself

and meet with, the right people in order to be more effective in your job, and the only way to do that is to put yourself in situations where that is both likely and a priority for you. Attend business meetings, professional association conferences, trade shows, college and alumni gatherings, and any other appropriate venues.

4. **Become a source of relevant information.** Build a reputation of expertise and being a sought-after resource. Keep your skills and competencies current. Take courses, and attend seminars and workshops. As you develop a following as a content expert, people will be contacting you, hoping to build a relationship with you, and thus putting you in a position to be viewed as a trusted authority. Building a name for yourself in your field is one of the most prestigious roles you can have. Once you develop this niche, you will become a person that relevant others want to know. Your network as well as your reputation will grow. It will also introduce you to people and situations that you may not have been exposed to otherwise. Having this kind of wisdom and experience speaks volumes for any professional.

5. **Always give something back to your profession and community.** Not only does giving back make you feel good on a personal level, it also brings you indirect rewards and benefits that you never expect. People remember acts of kindness and goodwill. They are then inclined to return the favor, as well as serving as a source of referrals and praise for you. Do not expect anything in return, however. Always be ready to help someone entering your field, someone out of work, or a young person starting out his or her career. You might also offer to volunteer your professional services within your community or a nonprofit organization. There are many ways to give back to your profession – pick the ways that bring you most joy. There is nothing more satisfying than getting a note from someone thanking you for having an impact when you don't expect it.

6. **Practice networking etiquette.** Remember, it's a two-way street. It's a constant give and take. Whenever you are networking, it should always be a partnership that is viewed as mutually beneficial. Both sides should regard the relationship as a rewarding one. One person should

not always be the recipient, so do not forget the people that helped you when you needed their assistance. Even if they don't reach out to you, initiate ways you can be of help to them as a way of thanking them. Remember, no one wants to feel used or that their efforts were not recognized or appreciated. Etiquette goes a long way, especially in the world of networking. Lastly, be sure to thank those who have helped you by displaying your appreciation in a special way, at the very least with a personal hand-written note or sincere email.

7. **Maintain your shelf life and develop an effective social media presence.** Develop a track record full of accomplishments and leverage them appropriately. It will help you vividly remember all of the things that you have done throughout your career, and can come in handy in marketing yourself within your organization as well as in outside circles. As you build your portfolio, it is easier to reflect on your history of success. Your specific accomplishments and contributions may be a way to differentiate yourself in the marketplace. Another

important method for doing this is through social media, but this requires being deliberate and mindful of how we are marketing ourselves, our differentiators and accomplishments through venues like LinkedIn, Facebook, and Twitter. It is imperative to have a strong virtual presence with relevant and appropriate highlights. Focus on cultivating quality connections and communicating with people who respond and interact with you instead of thousands of people you really don't know. Keep your profiles complete, current and updated. Request several recommendations and include a picture (or pictures) that are professional, appropriate, and leave positive impressions. The internet is forever; once we put something out there, it remains out there for a lifetime. Choose wisely and selectively.

8. **Create a networking database.** Make it formal and be disciplined about expanding and maintaining your database. In this world of sophisticated technologies, it is vital to have your own database established in addition to well-tended social media connections. Your

database should include all of your contacts, along with all of the ways you can keep in touch with them (home and work mailing addresses, telephone numbers, e-mail; Facebook, LinkedIn, Twitter, Pinterest, Instagram, and/or other usernames if these exist). Be as thorough as you can and keep everything current. The accuracy of your database will be a key reflection of your success as a "seasoned networker." Update it regularly and create logs of all conversations, with flags for follow-up. Your database should at the minimum include key contacts, colleagues, advisors, friends, family, third parties, as well as prospects to whom you would like to reach out. Make it your priority to expand it, and be disciplined and creative.

9. **Have a clear, brief message to deliver.** If you are trying to introduce yourself to a new acquaintance, be sure to have a crisp opening that will gain their attention and interest. Keep in mind that professionals in every line of work are getting inundated with phone calls and emails every day. Why should they listen to you, much less be motivated to engage in a conversation or

meeting? Make your message clear and brief, outlining a mutual interest that will grab their attention. Remember to include a reason that the person will benefit from knowing you. Be friendly, outgoing and positive; an upbeat and enthusiastic style is always enticing and contagious. It is good practice to plan on refining your message over time, as well as developing slightly different messages for different audiences. Always be prepared and do your homework prior to engaging in a conversation. Most importantly, have fun and show your conviction and passion.

10. **Don't ever stop!** Gain and sustain momentum. Many people make the mistake of running hot and cold with their networking efforts. They only work at it in when they can, when they need something, or when things are slow. The best results are achieved when you make it a priority, are disciplined, and have a plan. Set realistic goals for yourself and make yourself accountable to execute them. Use a formal system for follow-up to keep yourself on track, with specific goals and schedules. Again, there are many software

packages available to assist. Once you have a formal system set up for yourself, it is like second nature, and is worked into the day-to-day of your job and life. You see the results and reap the rewards.

You may be thinking that all of this relationship building is easier said than done, and yes, that is true. Let me emphasize very strongly that nothing I suggest or review in this book is easy! It's all very difficult when we are applying to ourselves. We are all great at helping and coaching others but when it comes to ourselves, it is much more difficult. To reap the rewards of personal branding and marketing ourselves which include positioning ourselves to get the jobs we desire, feeling energized and engaged in our work, utilizing our talents to their fullest and staying relevant and competitive in an ever changing marketplace, we'll need to put in the work.

Remember Neale Donald Walsch's quote, "Life begins at the end of your comfort zone." Part of this journey is stretching ourselves to new limits by getting comfortable being uncomfortable.

Meet Victoria Wang, Non-Profit[8] Founder:

I started my career in education then went on to the business world within the banking industry. I was an SVP of Market Planning for one of the major financial institutions in Boston and VP of Market Research for a major investment firm. After spending many years in financial services, I worked as a management consultant for several high-tech startups and other financial services organizations.

While working in for-profit organizations, I had served on several boards of non-profits and had a strong desire to give back. When I came to a new phase in my career and decided to stop consulting, I was looking for the next chapter. I was always passionate about promoting, supporting and empowering women and wanted to play a more formal role in doing so.

After much self exploration, reflection and due diligence, I made a pivotal decision: to create a non-profit organization that would empower women as I had always envisioned! And so I launched and founded The Story Exchange. My reason for starting The Story Exchange was to provide role models and inspiration for women through the medium of videos and storytelling on the web. My family escaped communism and came to the US. This country has provided me great opportunities to succeed and thrive as a woman, wife and mother… and now I wanted to give back by helping other women tell their stories and giving them a forum, to allow others to benefit and learn from their stories.

---

8   The Story Exchange (www.thestoryexchange.org) is a non-profit global video project empowering women to start their own businesses. By telling the stories of successful entrepreneurs from all walks of life and sectors, the organization encourages others to gain economic freedom, create the lifestyle of their choosing, and uncover their full potential.

Initially I wanted to make a documentary, but I knew nothing about filmmaking. I found my co-founder, a documentary filmmaker, of the project through networking and constantly asking people if they knew someone in the business. Through a "friend of a friend," I was introduced to someone at the PBS station in Boston, WGBH.

I learned it is so important to have follow-through, to be responsive and to be appreciative of the people who help. It always pays to say "thank you" and to keep people informed of your progress. Do follow your instincts. If there are naysayers, but your gut tells you this is the right path—don't let them discourage you. Be persistent—which I was! If you have "counselors" you trust and they are honest and open with you, listen to their comments. I had several people who helped shape the project, who asked provocative questions and provided constructive criticism. When I was fundraising, I did not get discouraged when people turned me down. I would just ask them if they know someone else who might be interested and moved forward.

I really believed in what I was doing and was very passionate about what I wanted and set out to do. There is a lot of hard work, long hours, and disappointment in starting something new, and the passion I have for my non-profit got me through these tough times. I have learned, if you don't have that passion, don't do it. My journey of self-discovery has led me to reinvent myself a few times throughout my career and now as a business leader, entrepreneur, advocate, woman, wife, mother, grandmother and friend, I continue to enhance my brand.

Be flexible and be willing to meander down your path rather than go in a straight line. Sometimes opportunities arise unexpectedly. Be ready to assess them, and be willing to follow that opportunity. You never know what may follow.

Let me get back to my earlier suggestion of thinking of networking as relationship building. As with any relationship that you are trying to develop, it's important to:

- Be yourself
- Make acquaintances
- Set your own pace

Start with a few people you have identified and create a plan for yourself. Be diligent, proactive and strategic with your plan. The key is to create your own formula that fits your style, approach and needs. Don't make the mistake of overwhelming yourself or focusing on quantity versus quality.

Use the following worksheet to help you get started and create a plan.

RELATIONSHIP BUILDING FLOW
PROCESS AND WORKSHEET

1. Who – Identify people with whom you would like to establish relationships:

   Internal: _____

   _____

   _____

   _____

   External: _____

   _____

   _____

   _____

2. Have a Plan – Invest time and energy into building these healthy and long-lasting relationships.

   Action Items:

   A: _____

   B: _____

   C: _____

   D: _____

3. Commitment – short- vs. long-term approach:

   Short-Term: _____

   _____

   _____

   _____

   Long-Term: _____

   _____

   _____

   _____

(CONTINUED ON FOLLOWING PAGE)

4. Execution – Nurture these relationships by implementing strategies that deliver high priority attention with discipline and focus.

Proactive Strategies:

A: _____

B: _____

C: _____

D: _____

5. Follow Up, Follow Up, and Follow Up!

Method, schedule, and goals for accountability:

_____

_____

_____

_____

_____

_____

_____

_____

_____

_____

_____

_____

_____

_____

_____

_____

Use This Checklist to Practice Your First P: Preparation

This is the most critical part of the three Ps marketing technique, defining and identifying our brand, and requires the most time, discipline and patience. If you do not devote the proper amount of due diligence within the preparation phase, all of your packaging and presentation efforts will suffer. It is a cumulative process that requires your total focus within each step.

Use this checklist to assure you have done all of your homework and completed the appropriate initiatives:

_____ Identify your skills, competencies and knowledge.

_____ List your strengths and limitations/areas for development.

_____ Keep a running list of all your accomplishments within all jobs, all roles, all companies.

_____ Be prepared to discuss all of your achievements, your interests, and your aspirations, as well as choices made.

_____ Solicit feedback and input from others such as colleagues, peers, managers, staff, vendors, clients, etc.

_____ Define unique characteristics and traits that differentiate you from your peers and colleagues.

_____ Explain experiences you have to offer that set you apart — and be prepared to tell these experiences as stories.

_____ Create a strong network, starting with a database of all contacts.

_____ Build and nurture your network; discipline yourself to gain and sustain momentum. Don't stop!

_____ Identify functional and/or technical areas of expertise and any specific niches.

_____ Prepare a clear and crisp message when articulating and communicating your expertise (practice delivery).

_____ Set goals for yourself — establish a mission with specific short- and long-term goals and objectives.

_____ Reassess and update goals regularly (every 6–12 months at minimum).

_____ Have a plan and stay true to it; be self-directed, focused and purposeful.

_____ ALWAYS maintain a positive attitude (and a sense of humor)!

Packaging

Create & Build Your Brand

Once you have completed the first phase, **preparation**, you are ready to move on to the second: **packaging**. It is important to remember and stress that preparation is an ongoing process that does not happen once and end. Plan to continuously be reflecting on ways which enhance your preparation with more knowledge, experience and discovery.

After you have defined and identified your brand, the hard work begins to create and build your brand. The purpose is to find opportunities that demonstrate and showcase your talents and experiences as well as build your portfolio, track record and credibility. There are many ways to do this effectively. Some are quite obvious and traditional; others are not so obvious and require creativity. Your packaging will reflect your style and tell your story in a way that allows you access to the various venues in which you would like to execute your presentation. Think of packaging as the many diverse vehicles and tools you use to tell your story.

Portfolio

For many years of my career, I spent hours reviewing other people's resumes in search of the right candidate for my clients – both as an internal human resource professional and as an external search consultant. What always amazed me, and continues to amaze me, is how frequently people shortchange themselves in showcasing their accomplishments, their talents and their contributions. Mostly it's because of a fear of "bragging," or even worse, because they don't even realize what they are due to a lack of preparation. But our resume (the most universal part of our portfolio) represents our history; it tells our story. When we read a story, we want to know the characters, the plot and the conclusion... and we like to read about the characters' journeys through all of these situations. We don't really care to hear a generic account of how *anyone* might walk through that kind of story; we want to know how *you* did. In order for the story to grab our attention and for us to connect to the characters, it requires individualization so that we can visualize what they are experiencing and contributing to the story. The characters come alive when we get to know them: their personality, strengths, vulnerabilities and motivations.

Your resume serves the same purpose. If it is a generic description of the roles you have held throughout your career, it reads more like a job description that could really be performed by anyone. It will not excite the reader to want to learn more and to meet you, which is the ultimate objective of your resume. Think of it as a teaser to solicit an introduction. It is important, therefore, to create a resume that tells a compelling story. The best way to make that story compelling is to market our accomplishments, articulating what we brought to each role we have held. What did you contribute? How did your presence make a difference? You want to stand out and apart in a way that is memorable.

> Find a resume format that works best for you, the one that you are most comfortable putting forth as your best effort that represents you well.

There are many formats to use when preparing your resume, and if you speak with ten professionals in the field, you will likely get ten different opinions on which format is the most effective. The truth is they can all be effective if your content is significant and focuses on your accomplishments. I believe it is important to find the format that works best for you, the one that you are most comfortable putting forth as your best effort that represents you well. Personally, I have always preferred a format that is chronological, with a brief description of your primary responsibilities in a few lines under each job title, followed by bullets highlighting what you accomplished in each role. I also believe it is critical to present a well-rounded picture

> Do not allow for a long lag time in between updates; it can be difficult to remember everything we would like to highlight, and more daunting to go back and recreate rather than adding and updating on a regular basis.

within your story by including education, publications, presentations, professional associations, board service, community involvement, or special/unique skills such as proficiency in a different language, as well as any honors, awards, or other specific achievements.

I have worked with many clients who struggle with identifying their accomplishments because they don't accept enough credit and recognition for their own work and/or minimize their value. Again, spending the time and effort on the Preparation phase allows us to reflect in a way that acknowledges and embraces these achievements with pride. Don't take what you have done for granted even if it was early in your career. At that time, it was a challenge involving new skills and knowledge. Packaging your achievements requires you to share what you have learned and created both individually as well as part of a team. One particular client kept saying, "But I really haven't accomplished anything!" That required me to challenge this individual to new heights. After a lengthy "deep dive" into all of his experiences, he crafted a resume that was not only eye-opening for him in recognizing his worth, but landed him several interviews, ultimately allowing him to pursue new opportunities both inside and outside his organization.

Always maintain a current resume, making additions, amendments and edits as they occur. Do not allow for a long lag time in between updates; it can be difficult to remember everything we would like to highlight, and more daunting to go back and recreate rather than adding and updating on a regular basis. Also, when we have invested the appropriate time and effort in our preparation, we have begun the good habit of keeping a running list of our accomplishments. This makes it much simpler to maintain a current resume, avoiding having to update it on the fly when one is being requested of you.

Many people make the mistake of thinking they only need a resume when they are ready to change jobs. But there are many times outside of job searching where a resume is required, including for professional associations, board consideration, universities and colleges, and other various institutions. In addition, many organizations want a resume to be considered for opportunities internally. You want to be prepared when it is necessary.

In the end, resume writing is very personal and needs to reflect our best self and represent our own style as we fill the canvas to showcase our talents and achievements. Employers are inundated with resumes in today's marketplace through a variety of sources, both traditional and non-traditional. Social media has created many new outlets and venues for finding talent. In addition, thanks to the world wide net, it's easier to find top talent who are passive and not on the job market. All of these factors contribute to creating a highly competitive marketplace with employers having a large supply of potential candidates. This is all the more reason to craft and maintain a professionally written resume that stands out apart from others. It is a key career management strategy for advancement both internally and externally.

STRATEGIES TO MAKE YOUR RESUME STAND OUT

- Regard your resume as a vehicle for telling and showcasing your story – make it your own.

- Focus on accomplishments, not responsibilities – include measurable results.

- Make it visually appealing – use a professional and current font with plenty of white space.

- Keep it an appropriate length – be clear, concise and crisp.

- Include a well-rounded, holistic picture of your background, experiences and interests.

- Be sure it articulates your personal brand – how you differentiate yourself, with specifics.

- Stay away from overusing buzzwords while keeping your experiences relevant.

- Highlight specialized skills and competencies that set you apart, with examples.

- View your resume as a marketing document: the commodity being marketed is *you*.

- Edit and proofread several times for grammar, spelling, and punctuation.

- Seek feedback, input and suggestions from others.

- Ask yourself the final question: would *you* want to meet and hire this person?

Take pride in the key areas you select to highlight on your resume. You want to put your best foot forward: your talents, accomplishments and achievements.

A resume is the most traditional and universal document to prepare. There are other documents that professionals in various fields may find appropriate and necessary. Someone in the creative arts may require samples of their work. Technical and academic professionals may require a lengthier curriculum vitae of their background and experiences.

Your portfolio, which is the accumulation of all these documents, is an important part of building your brand and keeping it current throughout your entire career. Don't make the mistake of not keeping your portfolio updated on a timely and regular basis as you progress through your career. If we wait until we need our portfolio to create it, then we will likely leave out a lot of important milestones and accomplishments. Be diligent and disciplined about keeping your portfolio updated and don't view it as just your "resume" but as a way of telling your story – what you have accomplished, the journey you have traveled and the mark you left behind.

Meet Anthony O'Reilly, CPA:

I find the term "job-hunting" to be unfortunate. It focuses on the wrong thing; a job description. "I used to be a VP so in my next step I would like to be an SVP," and so on. Perhaps this is because I come out of the public accounting profession where there is a glaringly clear progression of jobs to aim for. You start as a lowly accountant and take as many steps as you can all the way up the ranks to partner. In this typical "up or out" model, it is more than possible to progress through the ranks even up to partner without giving much serious thought to personal brand or career-building. You need strong technical skills, of course, and other things besides, such as an ability to sell business and be credible in the marketplace. But the path forward is well-defined, basically the same for everyone, and you either fit the model or you don't. In either case, it is clear what the next step is.

My own point of discovery came after 10 years of life as a partner in one of the biggest firms. I had done what I felt was a variety of different things within the firm, including taking a three-year tour of duty in the national office and getting involved in some things other than the day-to-day client service end of the business. The time came, however, when I was neither a brand new partner making his mark, nor an established partner at the higher echelons of the firm. To cap it all off, in the words of one of the partners I reported to, I had grown my business about as much as anyone could in this market and it was unlikely to grow further. And so, after almost 25 years in the profession, I came to the first serious moment when I had to re-think.

To say I had a revelation would be an over-statement. I remember sitting with my coach, Rita, and discussing things, factually. (You might say, just like an accountant.) Over a couple of different meetings, and some exercises to get me reflecting on what attracted me and what didn't, I created four different scenarios. These were not jobs, but descriptions of what I would like to do and why. They were based on my motivation and desires and not at all based on technical qualifications or even job titles. There were four of them because I imagined myself in more than one role. I had, for example, been drawn towards quality, improving the way we did our work and education, and I wondered if it were possible to combine these in some way. It did not matter that there was not a clear job title for what I was describing; what mattered was that I could understand why I was drawn to these and articulate it to others. My only guide was that these were the things that I had been most passionate about.

"Going deep" may not come easily but is critical. It is where your brand really lies because brand is not the label you stick over yourself as a way to package you; it is what motivates you and sets you apart. I firmly believe past behavior is the best indicator of future performance and when you are no longer in the classroom but in a real live-fire situation, behavior is what comes naturally to you. It is founded on your underlying motivations. This is why it is important to "go deep" with yourself. Good interviewers will certainly do so. I learned to be honest about my motivations and my passions and to see these as my brand. This ultimately led me to the best role I have had so far in my career.

As you progress in your career, it is equally important to have a two- to three-paragraph biography that is a narrative of your career. It usually does not exceed one page, and highlights major achievements, education and other significant credentials. Again, your bio should be updated and adjusted regularly. In addition, it's a good idea to have different versions, including ones in different lengths for different purposes as well as ones that are targeted to various audiences. For example, I use my long bio within my marketing collateral for a prospective client, and my short bio for presentations and speaking engagements.

Let me share a brief sample bio with you to give you an example of what a short one could look like:

JANE DOE

Jane Doe is the vice president of human resources and administration of ABC Company, a global leader in the design, market and sales of mobile apps, where she is responsible for all aspects of human resources, payroll, information technology and facilities management. Jane is a member of the executive management team and is also the company diversity officer. Prior to joining ABC Company, she has over twenty years of human resources experience with other technology organizations including XYZ Inc, Orange Company, Main Street Corporation and CCC Company.

Jane has created strategic human resource initiatives within these organizations, leading change, managing growth and cultivating people-centered cultures.

Jane holds a Master of Science in Business Administration and a Bachelor of Science in Organizational Development from American University. She serves on the board of Our Kids and is active in several human resources professional associations, as well as community organizations. Jane has presented on the topic of talent management and human resources planning for a variety of audiences and was most recently interviewed by Newsweek magazine. She is the recipient of the Mayors Award for her contributions within the community.

Writing your bio is a good exercise to capture the best way to articulate your brand. In addition, you may want to prepare a networking profile, which is a narrative of your key accomplishments followed by target industries, companies and positions of interest.

SOCIAL MEDIA

Preparing a well-crafted resume and bio organizes much of the relevant accomplishments and highlights we want to be sure to add to our virtual portfolio through various social media outlets. Our virtual presence is a critical part of our personal brand. With so many social media choices, many people opt to use different ones for different aspects of their personality and lives. They might leverage Facebook to see or share photos, Instagram for vacation travelogues, Twitter for trends and breaking news, and Pinterest for shopping. Select the ones that make sense for you and use them appropriately. The important thing to remember is that even if used for personal reasons, the information can also be viewed by professional sources and contacts. At the very least, a LinkedIn profile is one of the standard professional sources for job searchers, employers, recruiters, sales leads, and market information, as well as thought leader materials. Establish a presence on LinkedIn that is complete, current, and strategic. Use key words and phrases to ensure your profile shows up when necessary and reflects you in a positive light. Include a professional picture and belong to appropriate groups to stay current and to raise your visibility. Be thoughtful about people you follow and your commentary. Post remarks and valuable information on LinkedIn that offer helpful insights to others and that showcase your knowledge and experience. Request recommendations from several leaders, colleagues, peers, staff, vendors, clients and other key stakeholders that can speak to your expertise and personal brand.

In the global marketplace, we have four generations in the workforce and people working together from all over the world. Communicating with each other and establishing relationships is very different for Millenials than what some Traditionalists, Baby Boomers and even Generation X-ers are used to, and it will continue to evolve. With such diverse mix of demographics and different preferences, styles and approaches, social media is increasingly a branding opportunity. Take social media and your virtual presence seriously and be strategic, proactive and deliberate in how you use it, work with it and leverage it in establishing, building and articulating your brand. Remember that everything you put on the internet is a public record of your personal brand. So put your best self out there!

Track Record

As we build our careers, we create a history that begins to tell our story and establishes our credibility. Another way of looking at this is to put it in terms of defining and leveraging our track record, which is something many of us aren't accustomed to doing on a regular basis. It is hard to remember what we did from the start of our career to the current day if we do not record and track effectively and precisely.

Don't take any reminders of your hard work for granted! They all serve as a way to chart your progress and history and to provide relevant examples of your achievements as needed. Think of it as keeping an inventory, taking stock, compiling a snapshot of all the great things you have achieved over time.

Let's look at some ways of doing just that!

Keep copies of performance reviews, awards, authored articles, presentations and other testaments of your work history, track record, expertise and credibility. This provides quick access to relevant examples which allow you to showcase your talents, accomplishments and value.

Obtain written references, testimonials and/or statements from colleagues, managers, peers, clients, staff, professors, vendors and other key contacts who can attest to your experiences, skills and knowledge. Approach it as your own professional "scrapbook," including all of these achievements. Again, we tend to forget critical details as time goes on, and if we don't keep a copy of everything, it will be easy to overlook something important and/or relevant when needed. Think of it as keeping an inventory, taking stock, compiling a snapshot of all the great things we have achieved over time.

When someone offers a positive reinforcement of your work, this is something to throw into your "scrapbook." When you complete a project, jot down highlights of your contributions and add to your scrapbook. If you participate on a panel or deliver a presentation, be sure to keep a copy of your content in addition to the marketing flyer for those events. Print out a copy of all of your published articles in addition to keeping electronic copies.

In short, don't take any of these wonderful reminders of your hard work for granted! They all serve as a way to chart your progress and history and to provide relevant examples of your achievements as needed.

Meet Trish Cotter, COO/ Global Information Technology Operations Executive:

I started my career on a factory floor, in the chemical lab of a shop that made printed circuit boards. I counted myself lucky to land the job because it helped to pay for my college education, something I couldn't have afforded without the salary. From my first day on the job, I was ambitious. I wanted to go places. Even then, I realized the importance of defining yourself - who you are, what you stand for - in the business world. Going into that first job, my professional appearance was something I really thought about. So I wore dresses and shoes with heels - and ended up walking on my toes all day, since the floor of the plating area was a grate.

Although the chemicals ate holes in my hosiery, I presented myself well, worked hard, excelled at my job, and was promoted to associate engineer. That meant my own desk and a solid floor to walk on most of the time, and a new opportunity to show what I could do. I knew from the start that appearances count, but I quickly came to realize that in any job, others will define you by how you operate on a day-to-day basis, that workplace values are more important than anything else in showing who you really are at work, and in a broader sense, who you are in life.

The factory workers at my first job taught me critical lessons about diversity, respect, work ethic and teamwork while I supported their operations. The experience of problem-solving with them on a daily basis established my reputation and my brand. I was there to support them, not the other way around. At the age of 21, I learned life lessons on collaboration, innovation, leadership, teaming, measurement and accountability. These professional experiences formed the foundation of my career.

Some people start out in business with all of the elements of their personal brand in place. For me, the process has been more fluid and evolving. Initially, I thought of myself as an operations person, a technical problem solver: identify a problem, solve it and move onto the next one. I've since realized that my true strength lies in relationships with people: learning from them, reflecting on what they say, building on their ideas, and also providing them with my own insights as well as opportunities to grow, learn and contribute.

A few years ago, after two successful start-ups, I decided to take a more conscious, deliberate approach to defining my personal brand. I began blogging for my company, increased my speaking engagements and joined an executive COO organization to broaden my network. This process gave me the confidence to realize that my knowledge and experience as a leader and manager was of value to others.

I engaged a career coach, and Rita provided me with the tools to further clarify my goals and interests. Subsequently, I made the decision to go back to school and pursue a doctorate in education, focusing on corporate learning. Last year, I was a full-time executive at IBM. This year, on leave from IBM, I am a doctoral student at the University of Pennsylvania. I use social media channels to share my journey with friends and colleagues, and have a website to provide some additional perspective on what I'm reading, seeing and hearing out there.

Defining my personal brand has made me think more carefully about who I am and what I stand for, and as a result, it has helped guide me forward. For me, it has been a process of self-discovery and self-actualization, of becoming more of who I always was in the first place.

Another part of building your track record is being mindful of how you show up and engage, and the impression you leave. How we present ourselves to others will greatly impact our track record and credibility.

It's important to focus on the positives and not dwell on the difficulties. As we keep our professional "scrapbook," it is an opportunity to be grateful for the abundances with which we are blessed – to recognize our strengths and leverage them in everything we do personally and professionally. Optimism and gratitude are part of the process!

Be grateful for our talents, our successes, our contributions and celebrate them! Every day, take five minutes to discover a deeper and new level of satisfaction and contentment sprinkled with lots of optimism and gratefulness by doing the following:

TAKE FIVE TO CELEBRATE YOUR TALENTS

* Acknowledge successes – big or small.

* Celebrate accomplishments – step back and take time to enjoy.

* Express gratitude – be happy for the experience and the reward.

* Recognize victories as they occur – relish in the moment.

- Reach out to others – thank people who helped.

- Accept challenges – see obstacles as opportunities for learning and growth.

- Stay positive – attitude is everything, look at the cup as half full rather than half empty.

- Smile and laugh – inject humor daily, best stress reducer and energy booster.

Remember, our track record is not only created by what we have achieved but just as importantly by how we have achieved it. Maya Angelou said it best:

I've learned that people will forget what you said, people will forget what you did, but people will never forget how you made them feel.[9]

~ MAYA ANGELOU

POET, EDUCATOR, HISTORIAN, AND ACTIVIST

In addition to being thankful for and celebrating our own talents, it is equally important to show gratitude to others. Not just a thank you but truly and selflessly acknowledging the role someone has had in your success and expressing gratitude. Putting other people's interest's front and center and reaching out to be of service, initiating without being asked. Sincerity and authenticity in showing support and

---

9   LaNae', Trisha (2012). "A Conversation with Dr. Maya Angelou." Online. Available HTTP: mayaangelou.com/news/13/ (Accessed January 27, 2014).

collaboration to express your appreciation is essential. *Fast Company* published an article by Howard Jacobson in November of 2011 titled "Gratitude as a Business Strategy" focused on this very topic.[10] It discussed how people do a lot more complaining than showing gratitude, focusing on what's wrong rather than all the things that are good. It's easier to jump all over something that doesn't go the way we expected yet we take for granted when things fall right into place as we intended. It went on to describe how so many people from all different professions suffer from "Gratitude Deficit Disorder" and even referred to it as "a global epidemic." Jacobson challenged readers to "make a list of people you are sincerely grateful towards and create an action plan to communicate your thanks, with no hidden agenda," which inspired me to come up with my own which I'd like to share with you.

THREE WAYS TO SAY THANK YOU & EXPRESS GRATITUDE

1. **Send a personal, handwritten note** articulating how they played a role in making a difference to help me fill a specific need; taking time to include anecdotes, reflections and learnings that display the mark they left on me and/or the situation.

10 Jacobson, Howard (2011). "Gratitude as a Business Strategy." Online. Available HTTP: fastcompany.com/1796660/gratitude-business-strategy (Accessed January 27,2014).

2. **Initiate an act of kindness** to address a specific need or interest of the individual who made a difference for me, such as introducing them to a colleague in my network who could be a strong resource; invite them to a topical and relevant program or event; forward an article or link regarding an area of interest; and/or treating them to a meal to display my appreciation.

3. **Maintain an ongoing relationship and dialogue on a long-term basis** – don't stop after doing the first two but continue to stay in touch. Follow up and show interest in their needs and challenges as well as celebrating their successes. Relationships are long-term and expressing gratitude is a process of establishing and enhancing trust so that it is an ongoing give and take that will naturally result in meaningful and trusting relationships.

There were several relevant quotes in Howard Jacobson's article that spoke volumes to me. My favorite was:

Feeling gratitude and not expressing it is like wrapping a present and not giving it.

~ WILLIAM ARTHUR WARD

AUTHOR, EDITOR, PASTOR & TEACHER

Credentials

Even individuals need to develop a brand for themselves... Whatever your area of expertise, you can take steps to make people think of YOU when they think of your field.[11]

~ACCELEPOINT WEBZINE,
AS REFERENCED IN ROB BROWN'S
HOW TO BUILD YOUR REPUTATION (2007)

Build strong credentials as you progress throughout your career. In addition to gaining new roles and responsibilities, you must round out your credentials with professional experiences that extend beyond your position. Serve on boards, committees and/or volunteer organizations that will provide opportunities to expand your network, add depth to your knowledge and experience, and enhance your visibility in your profession, industry and/or community. What you learn in these settings goes above and beyond your technical or functional knowledge and abilities. Additionally, seek out opportunities that allow you to give back to your profession, industry, and community, and consistently make this a part of your portfolio. Not only is it personally rewarding to give back, it creates new relationships that can lead to new possibilities and paths.

11 Brown, Rob. (1997). *How To Build Your Reputation: The Secrets of Becoming the "Go To" Professional in a Crowded Marketplace.* Cornwall, UK: Ecademy Press: p. 103.

Education and continued learning is also critical. You can never acquire too much education, whether it's through classes, advanced degrees, certifications or various training initiatives. Being well-read and educated is an asset that will always round off your "package" for the better.

It is never too late to go back to school or to start going to school. As a part-time lecturer at various Boston area colleges and universities, I have taught students that range in age from 19 to 69. It takes a lot of hard work, commitment and motivation to return to school, but it is extremely rewarding. Let me share a personal story. After I completed my undergraduate degree in business as a full-time student right out of high school, I waited a couple of years and then started back in the evenings to earn my master's degree while working full time. About half way into the program, I started having my children.

At that point, I found I had to make a major life choice. I decided to put my studies on hold so I could continue to work full time, build my career and be a mother. I made a promise to myself that at a later time in life, when I could focus on myself, I would return to finish what I'd started. Fast-forward 18 years later... the time came for me to realize my goal of completing my master's degree. Although it was demanding, I would venture to say that it was even more rewarding. I now had so much more life experience to bring to my learning. I graduated three years later, with my children in attendance cheering me on!

Education is one piece of our credentials. We gain experience through different work roles, but just as importantly through experiences we build outside of our jobs. Get involved and be active – join professional associations and play a role.

Make a difference by building your content expertise outside of your job responsibilities. Become a thought leader and content expert by staying informed, understanding the best practices in your field, and keeping apprised of trends and challenges. Being well-read and This level of knowledge educated is an asset that will ensure that you are will always round off your sought after as a subject "package" for the better. matter expert. It enables you to achieve a different level of demand in your industry, and can give you a powerful edge in the marketplace.

Meet Patti Nardi,
Supply Chain Senior Director:

Several years ago, I found myself at a crossroads in my career. I had enjoyed a successful career with logical increases in responsibility and titles to go along with the same. However, I found myself asking questions such as: where did I want my career to go? Did I want to continue to climb the corporate ladder? Was climbing the corporate ladder even an option anymore? Did I want to step back with respect to responsibility, change course within the company where I was working, or blow everything up and do something totally different? The latter would essentially involve reinventing myself for the next stage of my life.

I thought of it as a methodical process and not something I could just blindly try to lead myself through. I started with a rigorous self-assessment in order to define what was ultimately important to me from a life perspective. This was extremely enlightening as it highlighted that what I would've thought was important ultimately wasn't of true importance to me. Once it was defined, I went through a process of detailed goal setting (along with specific timelines and dates) in order to set a course to attain my goals and stay on track versus meandering through time.

Many times, we find ourselves in positions in our lives that occurred because of a series of unplanned events or opportunities. My journey was a process of starting with the question: "what if I could do anything I wanted to do...what would that be and how would I get there?" At the end, the "how do I get there, how do I take control and make sure I get what I want?"....a plan and execution to the plan, was the ultimate end to the journey itself. Defining my plan empowered me allowing me to not only create a defined vision and plan for myself but also resulted in a greater sense of self and confidence!

Just as with networking, too often people make the mistake of keeping their heads down, doing their job, and saying they are too busy to be active in professional associations. I would like to suggest it is an absolute necessity to have a strategy that determines what your objectives are, and then to select organizations to join that will allow you to achieve those objectives. Determine how this fits into your overall goals – be specific, targeted and purposeful. At different points of your career, you will have different objectives that will play a big role in determining how and where you spend your time. Over the years, I have been involved in several different associations, organizations and non-profits. When my family and children were younger, these included a mix of professional associations in addition to the PTA and community involvement. As my life phases progressed, the organizations I chose to belong and offer my time also changed.

When I started my business, I knew there were three specific goals that would drive my selections of which organizations to join. These goals were:

1. To nurture and enhance my existing knowledge and network within the senior Human Resources field,

which was directly related to my overall career enhancement;

2. To build a strong network and content expertise within the career management/talent management field, for the purpose of expanding my contacts in these specialty areas and staying abreast of best practices, trends and thought leadership; and

3. To extend my network beyond the human resources field, providing opportunities to meet professionals in a variety of industries, disciplines and professions, including technologists, scientists, lawyers, accountants, marketing and sales folks, and other fields.

With these specific goals in mind, I selected the right mix of organizations to achieve them. In addition, I decided how I would be involved, whether by participating as an active member; attending meetings, dinners, programs and events; being involved in and leading committees; or serving as a board member and offering my time and expertise as necessary. If you are going to take the initiative to join organizations, seek out ways to raise your visibility by putting yourself in a position to meet new people as well as to showcase your talents and expertise (and acquire new ones).

Not only have I found the level of involvement I chose to be extremely rewarding on a personal and professional level, it has allowed me to meet incredible people, build meaningful relationships, and explore many business opportunities. When you are genuine about getting involved and focus on giving back, it automatically leads to great things down the road. Although like all good things, it requires dedication and focus, it's like planting that garden: you can't expect immediate gratification, but if you give it the proper care, you will enjoy wonderful blossoming growth in time.

The best way to enhance your credibility is through actions rather than words. This could include writing articles, publishing white papers, teaching classes and/or courses, speaking on panels, presenting at association meetings, delivering content at programs, as well as facilitating sessions at trade shows. Put yourself out there to continuously learn and add to your knowledge base and then be ready, willing and prepared to share that knowledge as a thought leader and content expert. You want to be sought after as a resource and go-to professional. Build a solid reputation as someone who delivers results both on the job and as a serious and trusted professional who knows his/her field.

Alliances

 Your credibility and ultimately your career are also enhanced by forming strategic alliances within your network – relationships that have lasting reciprocal value to both parties. Alliances can come in different forms and shapes. The most obvious are with the individuals that offer added depth to our experiences and knowledge, who can balance our background in ways that provide enrichment. The key with all alliances is to provide exactly that – a balance! Therefore, it is important that we are ready, able and willing to offer and share enrichment in return. The objective is to be a resource to one another and truly offer complimentary knowledge to each other.

Many times this could mean that we have different networks and can enhance each other by sharing our contacts as appropriate. It could mean referring people and opportunities to each other, offering a different perspective, or being a sounding board. Another possible outcome could be opening unexpected or difficult doors for each other.

We've all heard the saying about being judged by the company we keep. That is very much applicable to our careers. Create key alliances and partnerships throughout your career. Align yourself with people you respect, admire, with whom you want to be associated, and who can teach you. As with all relationship-building, be strategic about determining who these folks would be and initiate a plan to seek them out, stay in touch with them, and be a resource. Do not be lax about staying in touch with these connections and maintain focus on nurturing these relationships. Remember, it is always imperative that you are genuine and authentic with your actions... and it is also imperative that it is always a give and take. It is not a partnership if you are always getting or giving – it must be a balance of the two!

Meet Edward Melia, Management Consultant and Business Owner:

I started my career as an analyst working with a major global management consulting firm. I worked as a member of a multidisciplinary team that focused primarily on large global M&A transactions. My group focused on the human capital and cultural issues that are central to ensuring a successful merger: What are the capabilities of each leadership team? What will the new leadership team look like? Who should stay? Who should go? How will these two entities meld together? These were some of the issues my team focused on.

It was a fantastic environment for me to begin my career and hone my skills. It was also invaluable exposure to a number of other professions and disciplines required to run large organizations – and to plan and execute complex and transformative events such as an M&A. But most importantly, it taught me valuable lessons about assessing my capabilities and motivations, understanding what makes an organization operate, and the ideal place for me in the context of a coherent team.

I was fortunate in many ways. My colleagues were some of the brightest, most successful and well-respected professionals in their fields, and I learned many of the disciplines and process that I still use today. Our diverse client base afforded me exposure to many industries and I got to interact with people at all levels of the client organization - from staff and line managers to the C-suite. This built my confidence, extended my competence and gave me the foundation for what would become my personal brand. I also learned relatively quickly that the world of "big consulting" was not a good match for me, and so I left to start my next chapter.

Using everything I learned, I recreated myself as an entrepreneur and business owner. I took my acquired knowledge, my valuable connections, my growing professional network and my passion for technology and built a startup company. I refined and enhanced my personal brand and made myself as visible as possible – through public speaking, panel discussions, professional seminars, and volunteering – all of which helped me become a known entity and served to grow my company. After partnering with brilliant people who complemented my talents and finding some terrific mentors, I sold my company and led the effort to integrate into the new organization.

Since then I have recreated myself several times, and over the course of my career – as management consultant, entrepreneur, board member, investor, interim CEO, teacher, mentor, volunteer. I have continually refined my personal brand each step of the way. I have learned that building and honing my personal and professional brand has been key to helping me grow and succeed – and the process has given me the confidence to take on any challenge.

Other examples of important alliances throughout our careers include mentors, sponsors, champions and trusted advisers. Mentors are sounding boards, sponsors advocate for us, champions are our cheerleaders, and advisers are the people we trust to be honest with us. Having all of these alliances is an important part of managing our careers effectively.

In fact, there is a great book by Carla A. Harris titled *Expect to Win: Proven Strategies from a Wall Street Vet* that discusses these alliances in depth. She stresses that while mentors are a significant component of reaching our career goals, this is not the only relationship that will contribute to achievement in our profession. She goes on to explain the difference between mentors, sponsors and advisers as follows:

Adviser – someone who can answer discrete career questions, those that may be isolated questions pertaining to your career but are not necessarily in context of your broader career goals.

Mentor – someone who can answer your discrete career questions and who can give you specific, tailored career advice. You can tell them "the good, the bad, and the ugly" about your career and you can trust their feedback will be helpful to your career progression.

Sponsor – someone who will use their internal political and social capital to move your career forward within an organization.[12]

I have personally found it important to be clear about the difference between each of these relationships, and to have realistic expectations of each. Once again, be prepared to put in the planning and work that is required to build successful relationships with these alliances, as well as to offer your knowledge, resources and vulnerability along the way. I say vulnerability because whenever we push ourselves out of our comfort zone, we will be taking some risks that require us to let our guard down. Showing

12 Harris, Carla A. (2009). *Expect to Win: Proven Strategies for Success from a Wall Street Vet.* New York: Hudson Street Press: p. 101-102.

vulnerability can be a scary thing, but if we don't, then we are not authentic, and without authenticity, we will not be successful. That is the biggest differentiator between those who can identify, build and articulate their personal brand and those who can't – authenticity! Be authentic, show vulnerability, and put yourself out there!

Mentors play an essential role in your professional and/ or personal development. As you advance in your career, taking the time to mentor others with whom you have worked and/or managed is just as critical and rewarding. Having and being a mentor are two of the major milestones

> Showing vulnerability can be a scary thing, but if we don't, then we are not authentic, and without authenticity, we will not be successful.

during one's career and contribute greatly to establishing and building your personal brand. A mentor offers a source of great encouragement and support, while as a mentor, you share your wisdom and learnings with others. Both relationships give us access to people and resources when making difficult decisions or career choices, and/ or managing complex situations. The typical image of a mentor is someone in the workplace, but mentors enter our lives from a variety of venues, each offering different things that speak to our many needs, each offering wisdom and counsel in different ways.

In fact, it's important to seek out multiple mentors. Be your own advocate and initiate these relationships rather than waiting to be mentored. Find your authentic self and personal brand by identifying what value you have to offer as well as what you aspire to achieve. Seek out potential mentors and advisors as well as sponsors and champions for support throughout the different phases of your career. In addition, welcome opportunities to mentor others.

A FIVE-STEP MODEL
FOR DEVELOPING MENTOR RELATIONSHIPS

Step 1 – First and foremost, identify what you need.

Set goals and objectives that you would like to achieve with each specific mentor. Be realistic and practical with your expectations, being mindful of prospective mentors' time. Once again, make sure that you are creating a partnership that is one of give and take. Offer your assistance, knowledge and resources to your mentors just as frequently as you ask for their help. It is all about relationship building – what you put into the relationship is just as important, if not more so, than what you get out of it. Approach each mentor in a sincere and authentic manner. Be clear and concise in communicating your needs and expectations. Ask them for their input and feedback.

Step 2 – Reach out to a variety of mentors to meet diverse needs.

Establish mentor relationships with multiple individuals across many parts of your life. Mentors come in all shapes and sizes from all facets of our world – both personal and professional. They can come in the form of role models, peers, colleagues, managers, leaders, professors, teachers, family members, friends, relatives, coaches and other contacts. We enter into these mentor relationships as well as maintain them in formal and informal ways. The key is to be diligent in establishing and nurturing long-lasting relationships with all of the mentors in our lifetime. Be proactive and strategic by identifying mentors that cross all of the different paths of your career and enhance your ability to develop and grow both personally and professionally.

Step 3 – Create a strategy that showcases your value and keeps mentors engaged.

Identify your personal brand and articulate it effectively. Prior to entering into any mentor relationship, do your homework. Prepare yourself for the difficult questions a mentor will ask you and be ready for the challenge. Enter into the relationship confident and empowered. Conduct your due diligence: complete the first P: preparation before engaging with a mentor. Know yourself – your strengths, weaknesses, skills, competencies, interests, values and priorities. Assess your short- and long-term goals for your career and life. You also want to have planned out some of the second P: packaging. Invest in your education and continued advancement. Be active in professional associations and involved in your community. Take on leadership roles that nourish and feed your passion(s). Engage your mentor to help you navigate through this process.

Step 4 – Stay true to your vision and your goals.

Keep a formal plan that you update and visit regularly. You cannot stay true to yourself if you do not keep yourself accountable. While the association is not a one-way street, the mentee is the driver for any mentor relationship – it is important to be mindful of this and be diligent with your initiatives. Have a vision that spans over five years at a minimum and revisit your goals on a regular basis. Make changes and adjustments as necessary. Keep an open mind to new possibilities while staying focused on your track.

Step 5 – Communicate, Communicate, Communicate!

Keep the channels of communication open throughout the entire mentor relationship and beyond. Let your mentor know of your progress – your struggles, lessons learned, and successes. Be sure to give your mentor feedback on a regular basis by sharing the ways they are positively impacting you. Show your gratitude and appreciation. Be an active listener – reflect on the feedback you receive and incorporate it into your strategies. Keep an open mind and be flexible to new opportunities and possibilities. Accept constructive criticism and offer concerns. Don't be afraid to show vulnerability and take some risks. Open and honest communications will set the foundation for building a trusting relationship and rapport for both mentor and mentee.

Use This Checklist to Practice Your Second P: Packaging

This is how your preparation starts to exhibit itself and your plan begins to take action, creating and building your brand. The activities in this phase help you to showcase your talents and experiences as well as build your portfolio, track record, and credentials. Refining your packaging capabilities will equip you with the proper tools to access the important venues for the presentation phase. Be sure to complete the following tasks:

_____   Maintain a current resume, bio, curriculum vitae and/or portfolio – add, amend and edit in a timely fashion.

_____   Update and review regularly – do not allow for long lag time in between keeping it recent and thorough.

_____   Keep copies of performance reviews, awards, authored articles, presentations, etc.

_____   Maintain copies of other testaments to your work history, track record, expertise and credibility.

_____   Create and update this "scrapbook" regularly, providing quick access to relevant examples as needed.

_____   Obtain written references/testimonials from colleagues, managers, clients, staff, professors, vendors, etc.

_____   Serve on boards, committees, and/or volunteer organizations to expand your network.

_____   Solicit other types of opportunities that allow you to your expand network and enhance your visibility.

_____ Continue to learn through training, seminars, courses, certifications, and/or advanced degrees.

_____ Stay well-read and educated within your profession, industry and community.

_____ Create key alliances and partnerships – align yourself with people you respect, admire and can learn from.

Presentation

Articulate & Enhance Brand

Congratulations! You have completed the **preparation** and **packaging** phases, which now makes you ready to embark on **presentation of your brand**! I will take a moment to reinforce the importance of taking your time to complete the first two Ps in order to be successful with the third P. If we are not diligent in successfully progressing through preparation and packaging, our presentation will fall short and not be impactful. There are no shortcuts here – it is a cumulative process. We must challenge and push ourselves to do the difficult work required of us before we can move on to presentation. The good news is you will know when this time has arrived, you will feel ready to present and will have the confidence to start articulating your brand because the foundation has been laid. You are prepared and equipped with the "goods" to market yourself in an authentic and sincere manner. It will be second-nature for you, and you will feel comfortable, at ease. If you do not feel this way, then you may not have been thorough in completing your preparation and packaging. If so, take your time! Go back and complete it until you have reached that level of readiness to move on to presentation. When you achieve that level, your confidence will soar.

Keep in mind, however, that it will take some practice as you test out different ways to deliver your message, and your presentation will continue to evolve over time. Not to worry: refining your presentation is part of the process. Our presentation will change over time and depend on our audience. If we have our preparation and packaging completed, we are ready to present ourselves, and will be confident in how we choose to do so.

You are ready to tell your story, deliver your message and execute your plan. **You know what you have to offer** – your value-add and worth. **You know what you want** – your goals and aspirations are clearly defined. Now you are getting ready to learn **how to ask for it**! This is how it all comes together and you are ready to present yourself, to articulate and enhance your brand.

Message

Your goals for presenting encompass:

- Expressing your needs, interests, skills and competencies concisely and assertively.
- Clearly articulating both what you have to offer and what you want.
- Selling your own particular value-add and differentiators.
- Making meaningful and long-lasting connections and relationships.
- Understanding and assessing others' needs in order to effectively influence and support them.

Strong communication skills are vital, but fortunately they can be developed. Practice your delivery on trusted confidants. We feel more comfortable with our message regarding our brand after we have told it several times. Sometimes it takes several tries of tweaking it until it feels right for us. Don't become impatient with yourself because this is par for the course and very common. Most people are not comfortable talking about themselves, even after doing their preparation and packaging. That is why I suggest practicing on your friends, family and colleagues as well as on your own in the car, in front of the bathroom mirror, and even record yourself on your cell phone and play back. This will allow you to adjust, tweak and improve.

Listening skills are just as crucial, if not more so, than verbal skills. Practice active listening, reflecting back to demonstrate that your comprehension is accurate. It can be challenging to employ listening skills when we are working hard to make sure our delivery is strong. Strengthening listening skills, however, will yield the best results to ensure we are communicating effectively by focusing on the right needs of the other person.

THREE FUNDAMENTAL RECOMMENDATIONS FOR IMPROVING LISTENING SKILLS

- **Attend closely to what's being said, not to what you want to say next.** We can get lost in our thoughts to how we want to respond and may neglect to hear the other person's full thought. Avoid doing this by paying close attention, hanging on to every word that is said.

- **Allow others to finish speaking before taking your turn.** In our anxiousness to share our own thoughts, we may inadvertently interrupt others before they are done speaking. Worst yet, we may even talk over them, causing a breakdown of communication. Let the other person finish and only once they have completed their thoughts, take your turn to express your response. Remember it is also important to take an interest in the other person and their comments rather than focusing exclusively on your own perspective and thoughts.

- **Repeat back what you've heard to give the speaker the opportunity to clarify the message.** Did you interpret their comments accurately? If you reflect back what you heard, it gives them an opportunity to confirm or correct your understanding. This reduces the risk of misunderstanding and assures clarity of message. Phrases to introduce reflection include "So I understand

Find out about the person and their needs, understand the challenges they face, and uncover areas of interest to them where you can potentially offer assistance.

that..." or "If I'm hearing you right..." Putting your correspondent's statements into your own words demonstrates that you have fully "digested" their thoughts accurately.[13]

Active listening can make the distinction between communicating and truly having a dialogue. Dialogic communications is an exchange of perspectives, experiences and beliefs in which people can speak and listen openly and respectfully. It is two-way communication that seeks to ensure clarity in understanding and searches

13 Kreitner, Robert and Kinicki, Angelo (2010). *Organizational Behavior,* Ninth Edition. New York: The McGraw-Hill Companies, Inc.: p. 412-413

for the different threads in the discussion – identifying similarities, differences and other ways of relating ideas. Dialoguing is affirming and supportive, yet challenging and reflective. We can create strong dialogic communications in our daily interactions with the following **Building Blocks of Dialogue:**

•   Suspension of judgment: developing an openness, being aware of our own judgments.

•   Deep listening: paying attention, focusing on the moment, not getting lost in our thoughts.

•   Identifying assumptions: "peeling the onion" to get to different levels of understanding.

•   Reflection and inquiry: coming up with questions based on your reflection.[14]

Whether it is meeting with a new contact to enhance your network, your manager to ask for additional responsibilities, or a prospective employer in a job interview, you want to learn as much as you can prior to the meeting. Find out about the person and their needs, understand the challenges they face, and uncover areas of interest to them where you can potentially offer assistance. This will enable you to focus on those points of interest to the individual in your message.

14 Gerard, Glenna and Teurfs, Linda. "Dialogue and Organizational Trans-
    formation." Online. Available HTTP: visionnest.com/btbc/cb/chapters/
    dialogue.htm#31. (Accessed January 27, 2014).

Interpersonal skills are just as vital. Maintain a give-and-take approach, exhibiting friendly, outgoing and engaging characteristics. Build and gain trust. Be courteous and respectful in your interactions. Take and display interest in others' talents, accomplishments and value. Find common ground, similarities and differences as a way to leverage your relationships. Build strong rapport and long lasting relationships as a solid foundation – personally and professionally. Most important, once again, be sincere and authentic.

We can always work at developing our communications skills and interpersonal abilities. The rules keep changing with the technological advancements and resources that are introduced to us every day. Can it be possible to learn, master and get the maximum usage of all of these options all of the time? Probably not. We can, however, create a reasonable and achievable strategy that works for us and accomplishes our objectives. It takes discipline, time management and a focus on quality rather than quantity. Articulating our thoughts with conviction, passion and truth along with sincere expression can make all the difference.

Meet "Joe," Technology Operations Professional:

Starting my career as an electrical engineer at a major computer company, it was easy to see the path forward. Ambitious engineers typically made their way from individual contributor to project manager, then to department manager, eventually leading to the ultimate role as a lab director. In the 1990s, this path was clear. However, as we crossed the end of that decade, the power of Moore's Law and the Internet changed everything. I became one of those brave technology warriors, transitioning companies, industries and cities looking for the landing zone. Looking back, it's now clear that the landing zones were very different then, and continue to change with time.

At a certain point in this journey, I realized it was time to assess where I'd been and where I was going. I realized that I needed to step back and understand the arc of my career so far. What were the things that propelled me forward and how did those attributes relate to opportunities I saw in the future? This was difficult for me. I had to figure out what made me unique, what I excelled at and where I had gaps.

This process of connecting the dots between your own expectations, issues, and fears and the trail you've left behind is quite simply overwhelming. But like all new things, the process eventually took hold. I began to see brand take shape. It started as a fuzzy image but as I spoke about it with my friends and family, it became clear.

In my case, I realized I am an "extroverted engineer who loves working with people and applying technology in new ways to help people and society." That one statement took a while to put together, but in the end, helped me to plant a new flag in my career. I was on my way.

Your presentation is not only about how you talk about yourself, but also about how you are able to talk about the other person – their interests, talents and needs. Your focus is to build a bond with the person you are trying to influence, connecting in a way that allows you to articulate your message. You want them to want to hear you and invite you to speak to them. Having a willing and eager audience, not a soap box, is your goal. You want to truly connect and dialogue with someone where there is mutual interest and need. Reach out and a be resource to them.

Messaging is an important foundation for presentation. Be mindful and proactive in crafting your message. Keep it appropriate and genuine… and most importantly, keep it relevant to your intended audience. There is no "one-size-fits-all" message. What you select to discuss will vary from person to person as well as the given context. The quality of your preparation and packaging will allow you to pick and choose how you will engage depending on your audience.

With practice, you will gain confidence and comfort in determining what works best for you. Take the time to think it through and speak from your heart. Pay attention to your body language along with your tone and eye contact.

Much of our presentation is conveyed non-verbally and long before and after we speak. Take care in how you are presenting yourself completely. Posture, eye contact, physical space, handshake – all of these things matter and play a role in how we present ourselves. Don't overlook or underestimate any of them. Ask others for feedback on how you have presented yourself in one-on-one discussions, small groups, in meetings as well as in presenting to large groups. Practice, practice and continue to practice!

Your focus is to build a bond with the person you are trying to influence, connecting in a way that allows you to articulate your message. You want them to want to hear you and invite you to speak to them. Having a willing and eager audience, not a soap box, is your goal. You want to truly connect and dialogue with someone where there is mutual interest and need.

Remember: make sure you are clear, concise and crisp. Push yourself out of your comfort zone and tackle new venues to build your presentation skills and your confidence. If you have done your preparation and packaging, you have laid the foundation effectively. Now it is about getting experience in articulating yourself. Trust me, you will actually begin to enjoy it and reap the rewards!

Visibility

Being visible means putting yourself in a position to have many and various opportunities to showcase your talents, accomplishments, and value to the right people, at the right time and in the right forums. Don't wait for someone else to reach out to you – identify opportunities and have a plan in place to initiate and follow through. Some paths will be obvious to you, but don't play it safe. Challenge yourself by presenting your brand in contexts that may be out of the norm for you.

In all aspects of your career, practice professional etiquette. This will ensure that as you raise your profile, you also polish your reputation. When people are helpful to you, take the time to thank them and think of ways you can be of help to them. Don't only call people when you need them. Return phone calls and emails, be responsive. People remember and appreciate kind gestures! A lack of professional etiquette can burn bridges you haven't even begun to construct, and even worse, destroy existing ones. Both are disastrous career moves.

Always strive to leave positive impressions with everyone with whom you come in contact. Help people and do not expect anything in return. I once met a woman at a professional association meeting who was a visitor. She had not been to this group before and did not know anybody. I had been a member for many years and in which I had a fairly high profile. During the networking hour, as I was conversing with a group of people, I could see from the corner of my eye that she was standing alone. No one was speaking with her and I could tell she was uncomfortable.

I was speaking with a new contact that I was hoping to get to know better as a prospective client. As I continued to engage in a deep discussion with this prospective client, I could not let go of the nagging feeling I had of this woman who clearly was feeling left out and unwelcomed. It would have been easy to ignore her and go about addressing my own need to network, but I knew better. I asked the person to excuse me for a moment so that I could bring this woman into the group. We all introduced ourselves to her, learned about her and her company, and welcomed her to the organization. She went on to meet other people as well. I didn't think another thing about the incident and went on to enjoy the program. But a few months later my daughter was looking for a summer position in the healthcare field. I reached out to another contact of mine who worked for a healthcare consulting firm for some help. My contact asked me to have my daughter send her resume, which she did.

A couple of weeks later, my daughter told me she had an interview at a healthcare provider in Boston. The woman to whom her resume had been passed wanted to share a quick story with my daughter. That's right: it was the sidelined woman from the professional association meeting. "All of a sudden your mother reached out to me, introduced me to several people and truly made me feel welcomed," she told my daughter. "I was able to enjoy the program and had a great experience because of your mother's kindness. I would like to extend the same kindness to you and introduce you to one of my hiring managers for her consideration for an interview for her summer opening." This was another great reminder to me of how every encounter we have is a part of creating, enhancing and articulating our brand. Be kind, generous and gracious. More often than not, it does come back to us in many ways both directly and indirectly.

Presentation is just as much about our actions and behaviors as it is our words and commentary. Part of being visible is exercising the "golden rule" – treating others how you would like to be treated. Offer your time and expertise. Extend yourself, your knowledge and your contacts as appropriate, without expecting anything in return. Act in ways that truly exhibit who you are, your values and your passion.

Meet Judy Dumont,
Strategy and Technology Executive:

Having spent most of my adult life from grad school to age 41 at the same company, it was a major transition to find myself with a year's salary but without a job!

It had been a wild and exhilarating ride to be part of a company that was born with the advent of the mobile phone industry and came to a jarring end with the wireless telecom crash of the mid-oughts. I was able to grow and succeed with the company from a client services role to president of a $90 million division of a $200 million publicly traded software company.

The prospect of a new chapter was exciting and daunting – how would I stack up? What was I good at? What did I want to be when I grew up? The biggest questions were how would my experience translate in another company, and did I want to go back to corporate America?

With a year's salary protecting my back, I decided to take advantage of the executive coaching provided to me and to try and enjoy the experience. Having gone through a great deal of self-discovery after the death of my father and the end of a long-term relationship, I was intrigued to go through the discovery process for my career. I jumped at the chance to take any test to reveal any and all of my characteristics. In the process I realized a lot about what I liked, what I didn't like and what my core principles were for my career. I realized I most enjoyed being involved in something from concept to execution, and that I definitely didn't like to be micro-managed or managed in general. I already knew that I didn't like sales but now realized it was because the whole process intimidated me. My final set of findings was that I had developed a set of core principles: to always try to do my best; to the extent possible, to "do good;" and to deal with people fairly– to create an environment for them to thrive in and achieve their goals.

I wanted to find an environment that would allow me to thrive but I wasn't quite sure I was ready to dive back into the rat race. As a result I took a planned detour. I joined a woman-owned small staffing firm. It hit many of the marks I wanted in my next career stop. It was very entrepreneurial as I "ran my own desk;" I owned the process from start to finish. It certainly had the elements of doing good and helping people in the process. Oh and it also would test my sales chops because my income was predominately commission-based!

After a couple of years on this detour it was time to get back to something a bit more familiar to me, that used more of my general management skills. This time my process was a bit more wide-open. I was ready to explore anything, and I was excited to see where my experience could be put to good use. I had many conversations about senior management roles across a diverse set of industries. My search led me from advanced manufacturing shops, to nanotechnology firms, to a quasi-government agency focused on providing high speed internet to all citizens in the Commonwealth. I chose the quasi-government agency because even though I did not have experience in politics or government and I had never built a telecommunications network I felt my experience would translate. I realized my skills – bringing diverse stakeholders together and getting them on the same page, leading a team, and breaking a large project and mission down into bite sized chunks so everyone knows how their work fits – is highly sought after.

Fast forward another four years and I have passed a number of tests in this role. I have added to my skills and confidence that I can successfully lead teams, develop strategies and execute plans across almost any industry. And finally, I have become one tough negotiator and now I enjoy the challenge! My personal brand? I am a no-nonsense problem solver who applies practical solutions to achieve desired results in a fast-paced entrepreneurial environment.

Put yourself out there and stay visible in your organization, in your network, in your field, as well as in new markets and networks. Your visibility is also about your scope. Are you able to reach people and opportunities with a wide net? Again, this may require you to push out of your comfort zone and to be creative. Speaking engagements, writing articles and/or white papers, and participation in panels are all good ways to enhance your visibility. Seek out opportunities and don't wait for them to come to you.

In a time of technological advancements and easy access to resources and tools, it is important to create a marketing strategy that enhances our visibility in the virtual realm as well as in person. In a time with four generations in the workplace at once, we have a variety of levels of comfort and knowledge in the use of social media. While it is important to use social media wisely, it is only one tool available to you. Create a plan that raises your profile in person, in writing, by direct mail, and by leveraging industry resources, as well as maintaining a strategic virtual presence.

I had a college professor who once asked a pretty provocative question which I like to repeat often: "Is your network who you know... or who knows you?" Think about that question. People often believe that our network is who we know. I have learned, however, that it is just as much about who knows you. When I started doing speaking engagements, presenting at programs and conducting workshops, I did not realize the breadth of contacts I was establishing. When I speak at a conference that has 100 or more attendees, I am enhancing my visibility in ways that go well beyond the one-on-one introductions I make. If I multiply that by several presentations over many years, it results in tremendous enhancement of my visibility in my field – as a thought leader and in the marketplace in general. This has contributed greatly to enhancing my personal brand successfully. Raise your visibility in a variety of venues and enhance your brand.

Be Your Own Advocate

Another means of achieving visibility is to advocate for yourself, at appropriate times with the right people. Don't expect others to be the only ones who advocate for you. Know when to reach out to mentors, advisors, alliances, partners, colleagues, friends and other key members of your network for their support and assistance in spreading the word. It can be difficult to ask for help; you may not want to impose on others, or have a hard time expressing your need. The truth is it takes more strength to ask for help than not to, and people with whom you have built solid relationships do want to help.

Don't wait for opportunities to come to you. Seek them out, initiate them and go after them! Early in my career, there was a human resource position opening up that was a perfect next step and in which I was very interested. One day the plant manager pulled me into his office and asked me if I had stepped up to ask for the position. My answer was: "Well, no I don't need to, I'm sure they know I am interested." At that moment, he gave me a stern lecture on the importance of staking your claim for roles for which you have the experience and desire to take on. I did as he told me, and that was a lesson I never forgot.

When advocating for yourself, be specific and direct rather than vague. Most people need your direction to understand the exact ways they can be there for you, and it is considerate of their time to do what legwork you can for them. People will often ask me to let them know of any companies that may need someone like them. I much prefer when someone can give me specific companies where they are interested in meeting other people; it's much easier for me to determine if I have the right contacts. The other way puts much more of the onus on me to try to figure out the right companies, and then determine the right people.

Advocating for yourself is just another part of presentation. If you find yourself struggling to make a case for yourself, one specific request is to ask a contact to listen to you tell your story and give their critique. If you are stuck in your networking initiatives, be specific about what is holding you back and how they may be able to help. Avoid being vague and general in order to yield the best results.

In this competitive marketplace, it is not wise to put your head down, do your job, and just assume you will be rewarded for doing it well. We all need to be our own advocates and market our talents, accomplishments and achievements. It is not about promoting yourself in a self-righteous or self-centered way; it's about being ready to seize the opportunities to advocate for yourself when they present themselves, and having the skills to do so in a genuine, authentic, sincere and appropriate manner. Being humble is a good thing and is a way of presenting ourselves; it shouldn't prevent us from presenting ourselves. Find your voice and articulate in your own way. Craft your message, articulate your brand, and practice on people you trust.

Here's an exercise to help bring it all together:

- Highlight your three top strengths.

- Tell a brief story: What was your proudest accomplishment and why?

- Identify your two differentiators that emerged through the first two steps.

- Incorporate those differentiators in your message.

- Craft your message to articulate your personal brand.

- Practice delivery of your personal brand (again and again and again).

Meet Ray Hilvert, Sporting Goods Product Management Executive:

My company was asking me some very simple questions; "What do you want to do next?" "Where do you see yourself in five years?"

I requested some time to respond, wanting to answer the questions thoughtfully, and viewing this as an opportunity for some self-reflection and renewal. They not only agreed, but offered to put me in touch with Rita as a resource for my journey.

I spent the summer months moving through a series of exercises that included self-exploration and assessment, 360-degree feedback, strength insight and action-planning, and goal setting.

I found the process enlightening and my self-discovery empowering as I built a clearer picture of what I wanted both professionally and personally. I was then able to refine and better articulate my message back to the organization.

As an example, I realized that a big part of my brand is integrity and team orientation. I took these qualities for granted, or perhaps discounted them, as they came more naturally to me. Initially, I pictured my future success as being more reliant on a different vision of what a leader needs to be or do. But in the end, I realized that these strengths are what really got me to where I am today and have helped define me. And so I shifted my focus to becoming the best version of myself by amplifying and leveraging those strengths in new ways.

In response to the company's questions, I asked for and was awarded with additional responsibility within the organization that aligned very well with my goals and interests.

Only you can own your career! It takes initiative and focus to manage it effectively and well. Identify and define the terms that meet your needs. You will see the rewards and enjoy a fulfilling career that allows you to maximize your potential, development and success.

The only constant today is change, wherever you work and whatever your role. The key is to embrace it as the door to new possibilities and options. There are several positive aspects of the last decade's change within the workforce. People are changing jobs more frequently and pursuing new avenues as they uncover unexpected passions and goals. Traditional one-direction careers are no longer the only option. Our careers may change with our life phases, especially as people are living and working much longer than in the past. The newest generation will have a few different careers and pursue a variety of paths, and all of us are now discovering new ways to reinvent ourselves. How exciting to have no limits to the possibilities we may envision! But this is why it has become all the more imperative that we are **prepared** to talk about ourselves as a commodity, to **package** our talents and accomplishments, and **present** our value both inside our organizations as well as within our profession, industry and community.

MANAGE YOUR CAREER... ON YOUR OWN TERMS

- Explore all of the possibilities that are options for you.

- Don't settle; do your due diligence to identify the best one.

- Ask yourself difficult questions and be honest with your answers.

- Create your plan and stay true to it – both short-term and long-term.

- Allow yourself to try new things – don't let fear get in your way.

- Incorporate realities of financial constraints and set realistic expectations.

- Exercise positive self-talk instead of rationalizing why you shouldn't be true to yourself, or talking yourself out of an option.

- Get comfortable being uncomfortable.

Keep in mind you are the driver of your career and will determine what success looks like for you. Your vision is the ideal vision for you. Identify the path that aligns with your talent and value-add and that will offer you the most satisfaction and reward, personally and professionally. Establish and build long-lasting relationships along the way. Be sure to reach out to others for support in addition to offering yourself as a resource to your network. Manage your career... on your own terms!

Remember the *Three Commonalities of Successful Professionals:*

THREE COMMONALITIES OF SUCCESSFUL PROFESSIONALS

1. Know what they have to offer (Their value-add)

2. Know what they want (Have specific goals)

3. Know how to ask for it (Advocate effectively)

Advocating for yourself requires strong leadership. Leadership skills are always in high demand. Organizations want to tap into leadership potential from everyone, regardless of position, level or age. Unleashing and building your leadership skills is essential to manage a sustainable career. Leadership starts with inner strength, and through this book's exercises – from preparation, to packaging and all the way to presentation – you will have demonstrated to yourself and to others that you have that in spades.

The definition of leadership has changed dramatically over the last couple of decades. I believe leaders are not only born but can be made. Everyone has leadership potential and capabilities. There is no one-size-fits-all leadership style. Unleash the leader within you which starts and ends with inner strength. Know what you have to offer, what you want and how to ask for it.

Following are my *Top 10 Competencies of Leadership:*

Listening Skills. The ability to conduct and initiate dialogic communication. Active and reflective listening results in clear communication and conveys strong interpersonal skills.

Emotional Intelligence. Self-awareness (self-assess-ment), self management (self-control), social awareness (empathy) and relationship management (relationship building) define emotional intelligence.[15]

Action-Oriented. Lead by example and create a culture that enacts the values you espouse, and that is driven by results. Set precedents that give high priority to the learning and development initiatives necessary to achieve results. Ultimately, you must have the ability to develop the people around you, drawing out their capabilities and potential.

15 Goleman, Daniel, Bovatzis, Richard, and McKee, Annie (2002). *Primal Leadership: Learning to Lead with Emotional Intelligence.* Boston: Harvard Business School Press: p. 39

Diversity Awareness. This means endorsing an organizational culture that understands and recognizes the importance of diversity for success; embracing the cultural, social and economic needs and differences within this diversity; providing positive influences and role modeling; and promoting the value-add of diversity for everyone.

Enthusiasm, Eagerness and Energy. These three Es elicit positive attitudes and positive thinking in those around you, resulting in high impact and motivation. If you embody enthusiasm, eagerness and high energy in your everyday interactions, so will others.

Responsiveness to Individual and Corporate Needs. Anticipate the unexpected and be a proactive problem solver, taking into consideration the needs of your peers, staff, superiors, team and the organization as a whole with the appropriate level of urgency.

Sense of Humor. Always keep things in perspective, maintaining a grounded and balanced outlook at all times. More often than not, laughter can be a stress reliever as well as a team builder.

High **Standards of Excellence.** Set a tone for high standards of excellence; display behaviors that create trust and credibility; maintain the highest level of integrity, honesty and sincerity; be genuine in your intentions; hold a high bar for acceptable standards, expectations, norms and behaviors, and do not tolerate anything less.

Influencing. This is the ability to be a catalyst for change and impact results. To do this, you must understand the needs of all stakeholders, be able to rally involvement and participation, and communicate in a way that promotes responsiveness.

Proactive. You're the strategic visionary who's able to envision and anticipate future needs, look ahead and translate goals and objectives into strategies, both short-term and long-term, and see all possibilities that you follow through to execution.

Leadership skills and competencies can be acquired by all – given the right tools, resources, development and, most of all, the desire. The presentation phase of the three Ps requires us to tap into our inner strength. When you practice the three Ps, you are automatically building your leadership capabilities as well.

Confidence

Your "personal brand" is how you wish to be portrayed in the marketplace: your reputation and credibility; your differentiators; your niche. It will be the message that you deliver, the mark you leave with the utmost confidence.

Confidence is how it all comes together. You can be completely prepared with an outstanding package but if your presentation is marred by a lack of confidence, you will lessen your impact. The good news is, however, if you do the preparation and packaging phases correctly, you WILL build the confidence to assure a successful and effective presentation! Once you adopt a marketing outlook, you won't even realize you're engaging in what has become a natural process of self-actualization!

Believe in yourself, have faith in yourself, and with this newfound confidence, trust yourself. Don't be afraid to make mistakes – you'll learn from them! Trust yourself to take risks if you want to grow and achieve new heights. Every day is a new start to build upon all of your previously acquired knowledge, skills, talents and experiences.

Think positively and act with optimism. Everyone has insecurities and vulnerabilities; however, we cannot allow these to hold us back as barriers. Give yourself permission to recognize your strengths and leverage them. Understand what your insecurities are, acknowledge them and work with them. You don't have to apologize for having them or even feel the need to eliminate them. You may determine that accepting them is appropriate for you to move forward, creating strategies that allow you to work alongside them. You may determine that overcoming them is appropriate for you to move forward, and have to work hard and strategically to do just that. There is no right way to deal with our insecurities. It is a decision that each individual must make for themselves. Confront what those insecurities are and manage them in the way that is best for you to maintain confidence and achieve your goals.

Know what you have to offer, what you want and how to ask for it! Own your career, stand up and ask for what you want. Your work during the preparation and packaging phases provides the answers to questions that only you can discover. There is no one better than each individual to ask for what they want and truly believe they have earned it. In addition to your supporters, lead that charge and get what you want! You will have supporters who are key parts of your network, but only you are responsible for the confidence you project.

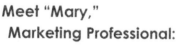

Meet "Mary," Marketing Professional:

I started my career in the non-profit world – first teaching English as a volunteer in Africa, and then working to help low-income individuals and those on welfare start small businesses in the rural South. I went back to graduate school and got my business degree, and from that time have worked in marketing in a number of different industries: automotive, retail, food, publishing and healthcare. I have pursued a bit of an unconventional path—always focusing on trying to find the best opportunity. And by best opportunity, I mean the one that is fulfilling my needs and priorities at that moment in time.

For me, personal branding is a dynamic activity. Because my needs and priorities evolve and change over time, every time I look for a new job (which – being in marketing – is not infrequent) it is an opportunity to reassess. What is important to me in a role and in a company? What new skills have I acquired? What have I learned since the last time I searched for a job? And how I can build these new skills into my refreshed story about my background and the opportunity I am seeking?

In my mind, personal branding is about knowing yourself, reflecting on these insights and applying them to fit your audience (the hiring company). By default, this also means it is critical to understand your audience and what is meaningful to them. You can then dial up or dial down elements of your story to emphasize what is important to them.

I have found that the more I strive to understand how my story can be meaningful to others and then authentically share that story with them, the stronger a chord I strike with them. Authenticity for me is the key: being honest with myself and doing the hard work to understand what I really want. To make it a reality, it is important that I put what I am seeking out into the world in an authentic way, so I share my authentic story with everyone! Finally, I try to genuinely understand my audience's needs and share my story in a way that helps them understand how my background and skills can contribute to the success their organization is seeking.

It sounds easy when I write it, but digging deep to get to this self-awareness is hard work. Ultimately I see it as key to my personal growth and happiness and in the end, am always grateful for the opportunity to reflect on where I am in my journey and where I'd like to go next.

Confidence requires this type of raw intimacy, honesty and personal empowerment. As we progress through the presentation phase, we may find areas we still would like to continue to develop. As discussed earlier, goal setting is an important part of preparation. Write down your goals and view them as a work in progress that is revisited and reevaluated regularly. You will continue to discover new areas of growth and development.

As you determine what those areas are, create a new action plan to keep yourself accountable. Most importantly, create a marketing plan for yourself that you will commit to at the beginning of each year and will allow you to determine the kinds of activities and initiatives for you to engage. Use the following Marketing Plan Worksheet as a guide to help you along the way.

PERSONAL MARKETING PLAN

1. Accomplishments of last 12 months:

    _____
    _____
    _____
    _____
    _____

2. Goals for next 12 months:

    _____
    _____
    _____
    _____
    _____

3. Professional association and community involvement:

    _____
    _____
    _____
    _____
    _____

4. Continued education, training and development:

    _____
    _____
    _____
    _____
    _____

(CONTINUED ON FOLLOWING PAGE)

5. Relationship building and networking strategies:

_____

_____

_____

_____

6. Staying current and well-read – industry, economy, marketplace:

_____

_____

_____

_____

7. Real and virtual presence activities:

_____

_____

_____

_____

8. Strategic alliances and partnership (i.e. mentors, colleagues):

_____

_____

_____

_____

By the time you have reached goal-setting, goal review, and goal adjustment as a branding and marketing outlook, it should feel simple, although it does take effort. Once you are confident in your value, setting goals that allow you to do what brings you the most passion is straightforward. It is also a hallmark that you have truly mastered the art of personal branding and marketing yourself!

Use This Checklist to Practice Your Third P: Presentation

This is how it all comes together, articulating and enhancing our brand! Once you are prepared and have a completed package, you will be able to present your brand with such ease and confidence that it seems second nature. Again, this level of confidence will only come if you refuse to skimp in the preparation and packaging phases – don't rush, don't cut corners, and don't be impatient. When you are ready to move to the presentation phase, you will know it and you will be ready for it. Your presentation phase includes the following necessary skillsets and initiatives:

_____ Strong communications skills – be concise and assertive about your needs, interests, skills & competencies.

_____ Exceptional interpersonal skills – maintain a give-and-take approach; be friendly, outgoing and engaging.

_____ Build and maintain trust – be genuine, sincere and authentic.

_____ Be courteous and respectful in your interactions.

_____ Take and display interest in others' talents, accomplishments and value.

_____ Find common ground: similarities and differences as a way to leverage your relationships.

_____ Build strong rapport and nurture long-lasting relationships as a solid foundation.

_____ Establish and execute proactive and strategic initiatives in your efforts to be visible.

_____ Put yourself in a position to have the opportunity to showcase your talents and accomplishments.

_____ Create your message and deliver it with confidence.

_____ Practice, practice, and continue to practice your delivery.

Epilogue

"Personal Branding and Marketing Yourself" is a topic that I am very passionate about as a career management and talent management coach, trainer and consultant. It brings me great pleasure to help others in understanding and achieving their personal brand. The mission of my business is to help individuals empower themselves to take charge of their careers and organizations to maximize their talent potential. I develop and provide tools and strategies to help others achieve this level of empowerment within their careers, which is what I set out to do with this book as well.

I believe everyone has the ability to achieve their ultimate vision of success and fulfillment. We all need support and help in getting there; however, defining where "there" is remains an individual question that only each person can answer for themselves.

I encourage you to embark on this journey with an open and inquisitive mind. Seek out the most and the best for yourself. Look to fulfill your passions, realize your accomplishments and achieve all your dreams. Be engaged every day in everything you do and don't allow yourself to settle for less than what you hope for within your career and life. There may be many chapters in your story as you progress through life and career stages. Challenge yourself to learn new things and stretch new muscles every day. Reflect deeply to ask yourself difficult questions and find your answers. Expect it to be very challenging and exhilarating. You've heard many stories throughout this book and now it's time to create your own.

Managing our careers and tapping into our utmost potential is hard work and should be approached methodically, strategically and proactively. Take charge and be in the driver's seat rather than sitting in the back going along for the ride. Do your due diligence, practice your three Ps, and you will drive a successful and fulfilling career. Create your personal brand and market yourself by:

- Making a commitment to yourself.

- Investing proper time, effort and focus.

- Being disciplined and accountable.

- Gaining and maintaining momentum.

- Enjoying the process – have fun!

I wish you much success and luck as you start your journey. Stay open to new possibilities and discoveries! Please share your success stories with me along the way! Enjoy the journey!

Interested in Engaging Rita's Coaching, Training or Consulting Services?

Rita B. Allen Associates takes a results-oriented approach in offering customized career and talent management coaching, training and consulting services to individuals and organizations including:

- Executive Coaching
- Career Coaching
- Team Coaching
- Human Resources Coaching

- Leadership Development
- Management Training
- Career Development
- Human Resources Consulting

Her goal is to work with managers, executives and their teams to build strong leadership capabilities and empower individuals to take charge of their careers. Rita guides individuals and teams through the entire career coaching process using a variety of methods including one-on-one coaching, assessment tools, 360 feedback, development exercises, action planning, growth strategies, and skills training creating a model that is customized based on their needs.

Rita's extensive network and strong affiliations within the business and human resources communities provide her with a unique mix of business knowledge and real world experience. Her authentic and pragmatic approach combined with her warmth and high energy contributes to her instant connection with clients and audiences. In addition to her coaching, training, and consulting work, she is a Lecturer at various Boston area universities, a writer, and a frequent speaker and presenter at industry events, conferences and workshops.

If you would like to engage Rita for her coaching, training or consulting services, or to order more books, call 781-890-6803 or visit www.ritaballenassociates.com.

I hope you enjoyed this book and I look forward to hearing about your journey. Please share your thoughts, challenges, successes and lessons learned along the way with me. I also welcome the opportunity to work with you and/or your organization as you continue to practice these strategies as well as discover new ones. I look forward to hearing from you!

Thank you for your support!

~ RITA

CPSIA information can be obtained
at www.ICGtesting.com
Printed in the USA
BVOW09*1707190418
513863BV00002B/52/P